hanley▲wood

**HOME BUILDING &
EMODELING BASICS**

W9-DET-078

THE ESSENTIAL GUIDE TO
EXTERIORS

FROM THE EDITORS OF

JLC
The Journal of Light
Construction

hanley▲wood

THE ESSENTIAL GUIDE TO
EXTERIORS

Published by Hanley Wood
One Thomas Circle, NW, Suite 600
Washington, DC 20005

Distribution Center
29333 Lorie Lane
Wixom, Michigan 48393

THE JOURNAL OF LIGHT CONSTRUCTION
186 Allen Brook Lane
Williston, Vermont 05495

Edited by Clayton DeKorne
Illustrations by Tim Healey
Production by Theresa Emerson
For more information on The Journal of Light Construction or to subscribe to the magazine, visit www.jlconline.com

HANLEY WOOD CONSUMER GROUP
Group Publisher, **Andrew Schultz**
Associate Publisher, Editorial Development, **Jennifer Pearce**
Managing Editor, **Hannah McCann**
Senior Editor, **Nate Ewell**
Proofreader, **Joe Gladziszewski**
Vice President, Retail Sales, **Scott Hill**
National Sales Manager, **Bruce Holmes**

Most Hanley Wood titles are available at quantity discounts with bulk purchases for educational, business,
or sales promotional use. For information, please contact Bruce Holmes at bholmes@hanleywood.com.

VC GRAPHICS
President, Creative Director, **Veronica Claro Vannoy**
Graphic Designer, **Jennifer Gerstein**
Graphic Designer, **Denise Reiffenstein**

10 9 8 7 6 5 4 3 2 1

Printed in the United States of America

Library of Congress Control Number: 2005932293

ISBN-10: 1-931131-52-X
ISBN-13: 978-1-931131-52-0

DISCLAIMER OF LIABILITY
Construction is inherently dangerous work and should be undertaken only by trained building professionals. This book is intended for
expert building professionals who are competent to evaluate the information provided and who accept full responsibility for the
application of this information. The techniques, practices, and tools described herein may or may not meet current safety requirements in
your jurisdiction. The editors and publisher do not approve of the violation of any safety regulations and urge readers to follow
all current codes and regulations as well as commonsense safety practices. An individual who uses the information contained in this
book thereby accepts the risks inherent in such use and accepts the disclaimer of liability contained herein.

The editors and publisher hereby fully disclaim liability to any and all parties for any loss, and do not assume any liability whatsoever
for any loss or alleged damages caused by the use or interpretation of the information found in this book, regardless of whether
such information contains deficiencies, errors, or omission, and regardless of whether such deficiencies, errors, or omissions result
from negligence, accident, or any other cause that may be attributed to the editors or publisher.

Acknowledgements

Several years ago, then Journal of Light Construction chief editor Steve Bliss assembled a group of editors to share thoughts on creating our own manual of best practice — the JLC Field Guide. We imagined this as a builder's trusty companion, ever present on the seat of the truck or in the toolbox, ready to answer the kinds of questions that come up on the job site every day.

Thanks to Steve Bliss, who envisioned, mapped, and directed the project in its early stages; to Clayton DeKorne, who expertly executed the work that Steve had started; to Tim Healey for illustration; to JLC staff editors Ted Cushman and Charlie Wardell, who compiled large portions of the original manuscript; to Josie Masterson-Glen for editorial production and copyediting; to Jacinta Monniere for the original book design; to Barb Nevins, Lyn Hoffelt, and Theresa Emerson for production work; to Ursula Jones for production support; and to Sal Alfano and Rick Strachan of Hanley Wood's Washington, D.C., office for executive management.

Finally, special thanks to all the authors and JLC editors over the years, too numerous to mention, whose work is the basis of this volume.

Don Jackson

JLC Editor

Introduction

Over the last 20 years, The Journal of Light Construction has amassed a wealth of first-hand, practical building knowledge from professionals who have dedicated themselves to custom residential projects. In the Home Building & Remodeling Basics Series, we have distilled this valuable knowledge into handy reference guides — selecting the critical data, fundamental principles, and rules of thumb that apply to strategic phases of residential building and remodeling.

Our intention is not to set building standards, but to provide the housebuilding trades with a compilation of practical details and proven methods that work for the many builders, remodelers, subcontractors, engineers, and architects who are committed to producing top-quality, custom homes. The recommendations we have compiled in these volumes usually exceed the building code. Code compliance is essential to building a safe home — one that won't collapse or create unsafe living conditions for the occupants. However, we are striving to reach beyond this minimum standard by offering a record of best practice for residential construction: details and methods used not only to produce a safe building, but to create a long-lasting, fine-quality home.

While it is not our first focus, we have made every effort to uphold the building codes. The prescriptive recommendations in this book are generally consistent with the 2000 International Residential Code and the Wood Frame Construction Manual for One- and Two-Family Dwellings, published by the American Forest and Paper Association. Although these standards reflect the major U.S. model codes (CABO, BOCA, ICBO, and SBCCI), regional conditions have forced some municipalities to adopt more stringent requirements. Before taking the information in this volume as gospel, consult your local code authority.

As comprehensive as we have tried to make this resource, it will be imperfect. Certainly we have strived to limit any error. However, many variables, not just codes, affect local building and remodeling practices. Climate variability, material availability, land-use regulations, and native building traditions all impact how houses are built in each city, town, county, and region. To account for every variation would require a database of understanding far greater than the scope of this book. Instead, we focus here on some principles of physics, design, and craftsmanship that won't change by region or style. It is our hope that these principles, used alongside the building code, will guide professionals toward a greater understanding of best practice.

Clayton DeKorne

Editor

How to Use this Book

This volume is intended to be used as a reference book for professionals and experienced homeowners with an understanding of basic construction techniques. It is organized in general order of construction, and within each section we have provided several navigational tools to help you quickly located the information you need, including a section headline at the top of the page, cross-references within the text, and references to Figures and illustrations.

Table of Contents: The two-page table of contents found on the following spread offers a detailed look at this book — featuring not just each section, but the individual topics found therein, along with page numbers for quick reference.

Index: A detailed index of the entire volume can be found at the back of this book.

Figures: When appropriate, tables, graphs, and illustrations have been added to help clarify the subject matter. Every effort has been made to place these Figures on the same page, or spread of pages, as the copy which references them. You will find references to Figures in bold in the text; in the event that the Figure falls on an earlier page or in another section, a page reference will be included in the text.

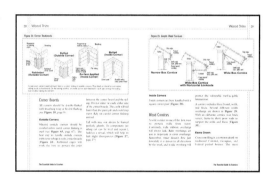

Be sure to pick up the other three books in the Home Building & Remodeling Basics Series for more valuable information that will help you get your next project done right:

- The Essential Guide to Framing
- The Essential Guide to Foundations
- The Essential Guide to Roofing

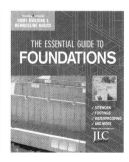
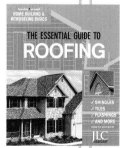

Table of Contents

Estimating Siding Materials

Calculating Wall Area

All siding quantities are based on the square footage of the house walls to be covered. Formulas to calculate the square footage of different shaped wall sections are shown in **Figure 1**.

To provide allowances for waste, apply the following:

- Do not deduct area of standard-size windows and doors;

- For openings over 50 sq. ft. (such as garage doors or large window walls), deduct only 75% of the total opening area;

- For triangular wall areas, add 1 foot in height to the original measurements.

Estimating Sheathing Wrap

- Asphalt felt typically comes in rolls 36 in. wide by 144 ft. long (432 sq. ft.), which will cover about 4 squares with overlap (see "Installing Sheathing Wrap," page 11).

- Plastic housewrap typically comes in rolls 9 ft. wide by 111.1 ft. long (999.9 sq. ft. or 9.2 squares with overlap) or 195 ft. long (1,755 sq. ft. or 16 squares with overlap).

- Smaller rolls of plastic housewrap are available at 4.5 ft. wide x 222 ft. long (999.9 sq. ft. or 9.2 squares with overlap) and 3 ft. wide x 111.1 ft. long (333.3 sq. ft. or 3 squares with overlap).

Estimating Board Siding Coverage

Standard board (wood) siding usually is sold either by the linear (running) foot or by the board foot. Depending on the pattern, more or less material will overlap when installed. To estimate the amount of material to buy:

- Calculate coverage area by adding all wall sections, as described in "Calculating Wall Area" (**Figure 1**), then multiply by the appropriate factor from the table in **Figure 2**.

- Add 5% to 10% to linear or board-feet totals for waste. Premium-grade material will have less waste from fewer culls, but the more inside and

Figure 1. Calculating Wall Area

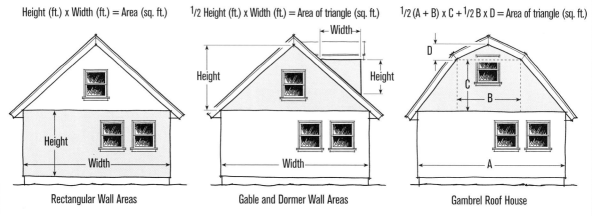

Height (ft.) x Width (ft.) = Area (sq. ft.) $1/2$ Height (ft.) x Width (ft.) = Area of triangle (sq. ft.) $1/2$ (A + B) x C + $1/2$ B x D = Area of triangle (sq. ft.)

Rectangular Wall Areas   Gable and Dormer Wall Areas   Gambrel Roof House

To calculate siding coverage area, add the areas of all wall sections. Include dormer and bay walls, porch areas, and entry alcoves.

outside corners there are, the more trimmed waste there will be.

Starter Strip for Lap Siding

- For clapboards (beveled wood siding), as well as plywood, hardboard, and fiber-cement lap siding, include at least 100 lin. ft. of starter strip for every 1,000 sq. ft. of siding material (**see Figure 60,** page 62).

Estimating Shingle and Shake Coverage

The same shingles and shakes used to cover roofs may be used as siding; however, different maximum exposures apply (see **Figure 43**, page 46). Also, manufacturers package their shingles for different applications — either in four-bundle "roof" packs or two-bundle "wall" packs. Both packs contain a square of shingles, and both may be used for siding applications.

As with roofing shingles and shakes, actual coverage on sidewalls depends on the exposure at which the shingles and shakes are applied. Refer to **Figures 3 and 4** to calculate actual coverage.

In addition to field coverage found in tables:

- Add one square for every 100 vertical ft. of corners. (For smaller jobs, figure one bundle for every 25 ft. of corners if material comes in a four-bundle square, or one bundle for every 20 ft. of corners if material comes in a five-bundle square.)

Figure 2. Board Siding Coverage

Pattern	Nominal Width	Dressed Width	Exposed Face Width	Multiplier for Linear Feet[1]	Multiplier for Board Feet[2]
Bevel &	4 in.	$3^{1}/_{2}$ in.	$2^{1}/_{2}$ in.	4.8	1.60
Bungalow	6	$5^{1}/_{2}$	$4^{1}/_{2}$	2.67	1.33
	8	$7^{1}/_{4}$	$6^{1}/_{4}$	1.92	1.28
	10	$9^{1}/_{4}$	$8^{1}/_{4}$	1.45	1.21
Dolly	4 in.	$3^{1}/_{2}$ in.	3 in.	4.0	1.33
Varden	6	$5^{1}/_{2}$	5	2.4	1.2
	8	$7^{1}/_{4}$	$6^{3}/_{4}$	1.78	1.19
	10	$9^{1}/_{4}$	$8^{3}/_{4}$	1.37	1.14
	12	$11^{1}/_{4}$	$10^{3}/_{4}$	1.12	1.12
Drop, T&G	4 in.	$3^{3}/_{8}$ in.	$3^{1}/_{8}$ in.	3.84	1.28
and Channel	6	$5^{3}/_{8}$	$5^{1}/_{8}$	2.34	1.17
Rustic[3]	8	$7^{1}/_{8}$	$6^{7}/_{8}$	1.75	1.16
	10	$9^{1}/_{8}$	$8^{7}/_{8}$	1.35	1.13

(1) To calculate the total linear feet of a particular board siding, multiply the factor in this column by the square feet of wall to be covered. This linear-foot factor is derived by dividing 12 in. by the exposed face width.

(2) To calculate the total board feet of a particular board siding, multiply this factor by the square feet of wall to be covered. This board-feet factor is derived by dividing the nominal width by the exposed face width, and assumes normal 1x stock.

(3) The exposed face width on board-on-batten and board-on-board applications will vary depending on material sizes selected and the overlap applied. Determine exposed face, then use appropriate factor. (Minimum overlap is $^{1}/_{2}$ in.)

Multipliers (factors) do not include any allowance for trim or waste and do not apply to diagonal installations. When multiplying factors by the square footage to be covered, add 10% allowance for trimmings and waste. See Figure 4-36 for examples of siding patterns.

Figure 3. Single-Course Shingle Coverage

Approximate Coverage (sq. ft.) of One Square (4-bundle pack) of Shingles at Indicated Weather Exposures

Length and Thickness (in.)	Weather Exposure (in.)												
	$3^{1}/_{2}$	4	$4^{1}/_{2}$	5	$5^{1}/_{2}$	6	$6^{1}/_{2}$	7	$7^{1}/_{2}$	8	$8^{1}/_{2}$	9	$9^{1}/_{2}$
16x5/2	70	80	90	100	110	120	130	140	150	160	170	180	190
18x5/$2^{1}/_{4}$	–	$72^{1}/_{2}$	$81^{1}/_{2}$	$90^{1}/_{2}$	100	109	118	127	136	$145^{1}/_{2}$	$154^{1}/_{2}$	$163^{1}/_{2}$	$172^{1}/_{2}$
24x4/2	–	–	–	–	$73^{1}/_{2}$	80	$86^{1}/_{2}$	93	100	$106^{1}/_{2}$	113	120	$126^{1}/_{2}$
	10	$10^{1}/_{2}$	11	$11^{1}/_{2}$	12	$12^{1}/_{2}$	13	$13^{1}/_{2}$	14	$14^{1}/_{2}$	15	$15^{1}/_{2}$	16
16x5/2	200	210	220	230	240	–	–	–	–	–	–	–	–
18x7/$2^{1}/_{4}$	$181^{1}/_{2}$	191	2002	209	218	227	236	$245^{1}/_{2}$	$254^{1}/_{2}$	–	–	–	–
24x4/2	133	140	$146^{1}/_{2}$	$15^{3}/_{4}$	160	$166^{1}/_{2}$	173	180	$186^{1}/_{2}$	193	200	$206^{1}/_{2}$	213

To calculate quantity of shingles needed: 1) calculate total area to be sided (see **Figure 1**); 2) subtract area of openings greater than 50 sq. ft.; 3) add 5% of adjusted total area for waste; 4) select nearest approximate coverage for the shingle size to be used; 5) divide by 100 to find number of squares of material needed for the job. For double-course applications, divide by 50 to calculate actual squares needed.

Adapted from Cedar Shake and Shingle Bureau

- Do not subtract area of openings unless their area is greater than 50 sq. ft.
- Add an additional 5% for waste.
- For starter courses, add one square for every 120 lin. ft. of wall skirt for single-course applications, or one square for every 60 lin. ft. of wall skirt for double-course applications.

Starter Course

The underlying course can be either the No. 1 grade product used on the outer course or a lower-grade product.

Starter Course for Shingles and Shakes

Starter strip is not recommended for shingle and shake siding. Use a starter course of shingles instead (see "Starter Course," page 47). A lower-quality

Figure 4. Single-Course Shake Coverage

Weather Exposures (in.):	7	8½	10	11½	14	16	18	20
Shake Type, Length and Thickness (in.)								
18x½ Handsplit and Resawn Mediums[1]	70	85	100	115	140[3]	–	–	–
18x¾ Handsplit and Resawn Heavies[1]	70	85[2]	100	115	140[3]	–	–	–
No. 1 18 Handsplit and Resawn	70	85[2]	100	115[2]	140	160	180	200[3]
24x½ Handsplit and Resawn Mediums	70	85	100	115[2]	140	160	180	200[3]
24x¾ Handsplit and Resawn Heavies	70	85	100	115[2]	140	160	180	200[3]
No. 1 24 Taper-Sawn	70.	85	100	115[2]	140	160	180	200[3]
24x½ Tapersplit	70	85	100	115[2]	140	160	180	200[3]
18x⅜ True-Edge Straight-Split[4]	50[2]	60	71	82	100[3]	–	–	–
18x⅜ Straight-Split[5]	82	100[2]	118	135	165[3]	–	–	–
24x⅜ Straight-Split	70	85	100	115[2]	140	160	180	200[3]

(1) Six bundles will cover 100 sq. ft. wall area at 8½-in. exposure. Seven bundles will cover 100 sq. ft. at 7½-in. weather exposure.
(2) Maximum recommended weather exposure for single-coursed wall construction.
(3) Maximum recommended weather exposure for double-coursed wall construction.
(4) Four-bundle square.
(5) Five-bundle square.

To calculate quantity of shakes needed: 1) calculate total area on building to be sided (see **Figure 1,** page 2); 2) subtract openings greater than 50 sq. ft. from total area; 3) add 5% of adjusted total area for waste; 4) select nearest approximate coverage for the shingle size to be used; and 5) divide by 100 to find number of squares of material needed for the job. For double-course applications, divide by 50 to calculate actual squares needed.

Adapted from Cedar Shake and Shingle Bureau

shingle grade, such as No. 3 Black Label or No. 4 undercoursing, is a suitable starter course for sidewall shingles and shakes. Note: This means that double-course shingle and shake applications start with three courses.

Estimating Hardboard

Coverage for hardboard and plywood lap siding varies with board width and exposure. Follow the manufacturer's guidelines. An approximate guide to the amount of lap material needed for a given area of wall is shown in **Figure 5**.

Estimating Nail Quantities

Horizontal Siding

Order 1 lb. for each nail penny (d) per 1,000 sq. ft. of siding required:

- For 6d nails, order 6 lb. of nails per square of material
- For 8d nails, order 8 lb. of nails per square
- For 10d nails, order 10 lb. of nails per square

Figure 5. Hardboard Siding Coverage

Siding Width (in.)	Exposure (in.)	Siding Qty. per 1,000 sq. ft. of Wall
12	11	1,150 sq. ft.
12	10 1/2	1,200 sq. ft.
9	8	1,185 sq. ft.
9	7 1/2	1,260 sq. ft.
6	5	1,320 sq. ft.
6	4 1/2	1,460 sq. ft.

Hardboard and plywood lap siding varies by width and overlap. For various board sizes and exposures, order the square feet of siding shown for every 1,000 sq. ft. of wall area.

Vertical Board-and-Batten

Order 2 lb. for each nail penny (d) per 1,000 sq. ft. of siding required:

- For 8d nails, order 16 lbs. nails per square of material
- For 10d nails, order 20 lbs. nails per square

Shingles and Shakes

Order 2 lb. for each nail penny (d) per 1,000 sq. ft. of siding required:

- For 6d nails, order 12 lbs. nails per square of material
- For 8d nails, order 16 lbs. nails per square

Figure 6. Estimating Siding Accessories

Figure 6. Estimating Siding Accessories

	Amt. Required per 1,000 sq. ft. of Siding
Starter strip	100 lin. ft.
J-Trim[1]	200 lin. ft.
Utility trim[1]	30 lin. ft.
H-Trim[2], 12 in.	60 pieces
H-Trim[2], 9 3/8 in.	80 pieces

(1) Typically available in 12-ft. lengths
(2) Available to cover butt joints between hardboard panels (see **Figure 64**, page 66)

Vinyl, metal, and hardboard siding require trim accessories, such as those listed in this table. Check with the siding manufacturer for its suggested siding trim package.

Estimating Vinyl Siding Coverage

When estimating vinyl siding quantities, add up square footage (see "Calculating Wall Area," page 1), and add 10% for waste. As with wood siding estimates, do not deduct the area of windows and doors. This will provide an allowance for waste. If the window and door areas are over 50 sq. ft. (such as garage doors or sliding glass doors), deduct 75% of the total openings. For dormers and gable-end walls, add 1 ft. in height to the original measurements to allow for waste.

Figure 7. Estimating Stucco Materials

	Materials for 100 sq. yd. of Wall	
Type of Construction	**Lath (sq. yd.)**	**Other Materials**
Metal lath on wood studs	105	8 lbs. self-furring nails or 15 lbs. staples
Metal lath on steel studs	105	10 lbs. tie wire, 1,000 lin. ft. of 3/4-in. channel

		Stucco for 100 sq. ft. of Wall	
		1:3 Mortar Materials	
Stucco Thickness (in.)	**Stucco Amt. (cu. ft.)**	**Cement (cu. ft.)**	**Sand (cu. ft.)**
1/4	2.08	0.68	2.06
3/8	3.13	1.03	3.10
1/2	4.17	1.37	4.12
5/8	5.21	1.71	5.15
3/4	6.25	2.06	6.18
1	8.33	2.74	8.24

Estimating Siding Accessories

Add up lin. feet of outside and inside corners needed, and add 10% for waste. Include other trim accessories, as shown in **Figure 6**.

Estimating Stucco

Three-coat stucco requires lath as well as cement-mortar stucco. **Figure 7** provides some rough measures of the materials required for different construction elements and stucco thicknesses.

Estimating Brick Veneer

Brick sizes vary widely, and so do the costs. When estimating and pricing brick, keep in mind that larger brick may cost more per unit, but it takes far fewer units to complete a job, and the job will require less sand and mortar.

To estimate the number of brick per 100 sq. ft. of wall, refer to **Figure 8**. Or use the following formula (for standard 8x2¼x3¾ brick with a standard ⅜-in. mortar joint):

1 SQUARE FOOT OF WALL = 6.8 BRICK
WALL HEIGHT (FT.) X WALL LENGTH
(FT.) X 6.8 = TOTAL BRICK NEEDED

Figure 8. Brick Veneer Coverage (per 100 sq. ft.)

Mortar Joint (in.)	Brick	Wall Ties	Mortar Required (cu. ft.)
¼	698	23	4.48
⅜	680	22	6.56
½	635	21	8.34
⅝	590	19	10.52
¾	549	18	12.60

"Mortar Required" assumes 20% waste for all head and bed joints. The brick size assumed is 8x2¼x3¾ in. No waste is included for brick.

Sheathing Wrap and Flashing

All sidings will leak. Most water that leaks behind the siding is driven by rain or wicks into small cracks. Caulks and sealants are not an answer to stopping water penetration. Instead, all siding materials should be applied over a drainage plane (also called a rain screen) to allow water to fall down and out. This drainage plane is created by first applying sheathing wrap and flashings — lapped to shed water — and then by creating an air space and weep holes so water can drain away from the building (**Figure 9**).

Sheathing Wrap Materials

Sheathing wraps that work well include asphalt-saturated felt and plastic housewraps.

Type D kraft paper (a lighter black paper than asphalt felt), sisal kraft paper (asphalt sandwiched between two layers of kraft paper), and cross-laminated plastic housewraps all perform poorly in rainy and snowy climates. However, two layers of Type D paper work well beneath stucco in most climates (see "Stucco: Drainage Plane," page 70).

All sheathing wrap must be integrated with flashing materials. It's not enough to wrap a house, and then to

Figure 9. Drainage Plane

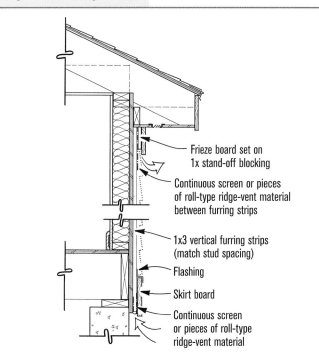

Frieze board set on 1x stand-off blocking

Continuous screen or pieces of roll-type ridge-vent material between furring strips

1x3 vertical furring strips (match stud spacing)

Flashing

Skirt board

Continuous screen or pieces of roll-type ridge-vent material

Siding that is pressed up tight against sheathing (even with felt or plastic housewrap) will retain moisture, causing the siding and finish to fail prematurely and water to move into walls. All siding should be installed over battens that create an air space behind the siding so water can drain down and out.

Figure 10. Sheathing Wrap Details

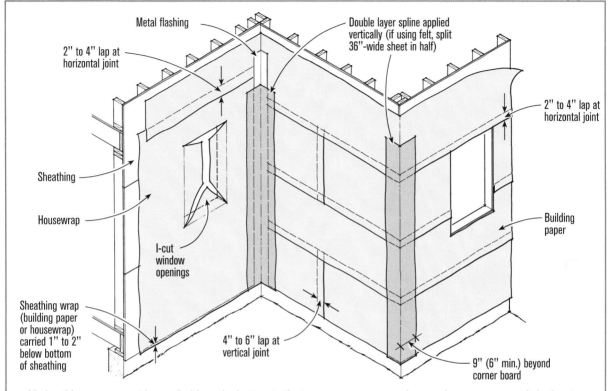

Metal flashing

2" to 4" lap at horizontal joint

Double layer spline applied vertically (if using felt, split 36"-wide sheet in half)

2" to 4" lap at horizontal joint

Sheathing

Housewrap

I-cut window openings

Building paper

Sheathing wrap (building paper or housewrap) carried 1" to 2" below bottom of sheathing

4" to 6" lap at vertical joint

9" (6" min.) beyond corner board

All sheathing wraps must be applied from the bottom to the top, so upper courses lap over lower courses and shed water away from the house. Always carry the sheet around corners, then reinforce the barrier at the corner by applying a second layer, or spline. This spline should extend at least 6 in. beyond the joint between the siding and corner boards.

simply X-cut the openings and fold the flaps inside. Follow the guidelines in **Figure 10** when installing any sheathing wrap.

Asphalt-Saturated Felt

Commonly available in two weights, asphalt felt, or "black paper," is made from recycled corrugated papers mixed with sawdust and an asphalt resin. When it actually was made from cotton

felt, 15-lb. felt weighed 15 pounds per square, and 30-lb. felt weighed 30 pounds per square. These days, asphalt felt weighs considerably less (between 6 and 12 pounds per square) and is now simply designated No. 15 and No. 30.

When choosing No. 15 felt, look for material rated ASTM D4869 or ASTM D229. The better material is rated by the more stringent ASTM

D229 standard, which ensures a weight of at least 11.5 lbs. per square.

The biggest drawback to using asphalt felt as a sheathing wrap is that it's difficult to apply well on walls. Generally, wrinkles are not a problem, but tears — particularly at inside corners — should be avoided. Also, try to prevent sags between the relatively narrow (36-in.) courses.

Plastic Housewrap

In cold temperatures, plastic housewraps stay more flexible than paper and felt wraps. Also, plastic housewraps resist tearing, so they are easier to apply.

Plastic housewraps typically are made of polyolefin fabric — either polyethylene or polypropylene. The primary difference in housewraps is whether or not they are perforated:

- **Perforated** products are made from a vapor-tight plastic, and then needle-punched to allow the wrap to "breathe" (allow vapor to pass through). Unfortunately, these holes also allow liquid water to seep through, particularly when the siding is pressed tight against it. The housewrap will slow the seepage but will not block it entirely.

- **Non-perforated** housewraps are made from a plastic fiber that allows vapor to pass between the fibers. These generally perform much better than perforated products at resisting liquid water, which should be considered their primary task. Relatively few houses suffer from water vapor penetrating from outside, but many suffer from rain and snow infiltration.

Figure 11. Sill Flashing Details

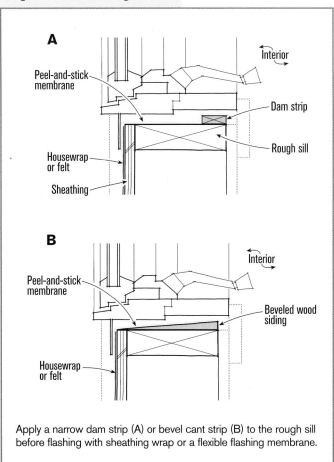

Apply a narrow dam strip (A) or bevel cant strip (B) to the rough sill before flashing with sheathing wrap or a flexible flashing membrane.

Leaching

Housewraps are susceptible to damage from extractives that can leach from wood siding materials, particularly cedar and redwood. This can be prevented in two ways:

- Install siding on battens to create an air gap, which reduces contact between the sheathing wrap and siding (**Figure 9,** page 8).

- Back-prime all wood siding materials. This reduces leaching and blocks moisture from moving through the siding and blistering the finish (see "Finishes," page 103).

Installing Sheathing Wrap

The primary purpose of housewrap is to stop water, not air. Air-sealing and vapor control are secondary. See **Figure 10**, page 9, for details about how to lap sheathing wrap to shed water.

- Use sheathing wrap or felt paper on all houses, no matter what kind of siding is used.

- The wrap should be continuous; avoid a patchwork of small pieces. Review flashing details (pages 17-20), as some flashings (such as those around electrical fixtures, mechanical penetrations, etc.)

Figure 12. Window Splines

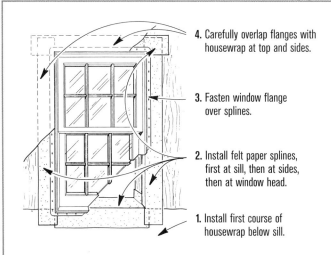

4. Carefully overlap flanges with housewrap at top and sides.

3. Fasten window flange over splines.

2. Install felt paper splines, first at sill, then at sides, then at window head.

1. Install first course of housewrap below sill.

Flash windows and doors with window splines cut from felt paper or flexible flashing. Make sure the sheathing wrap laps over the splines at the top and sides. At the sill, however, the bottom end of the spline and the sill flashing should overlap the sheathing wrap.

should be installed concurrent with sheathing wrap.

- Lap upper courses of housewrap over lower courses 4 in. and lap vertical seams 12 in. Code requires a horizontal lap of only 2 in. and a vertical lap of 6 in., but water may still back up beyond these minimal overlaps.

- Do not X-cut sheathing wrap at openings. Instead, I-cut the sheathing wrap, running the knife along the rough opening at the head and sill, and then slitting vertically in the center of the opening (see **Figure 10**, page 9).

Figure 13. Window Head Flashing

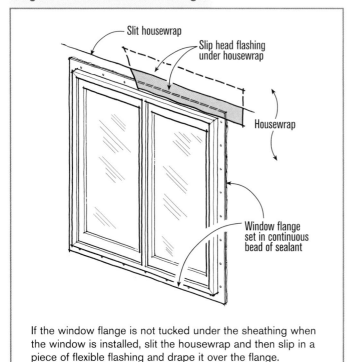

Slit housewrap

Slip head flashing
under housewrap

Housewrap

Window flange
set in continuous
bead of sealant

If the window flange is not tucked under the sheathing when
the window is installed, slit the housewrap and then slip in a
piece of flexible flashing and drape it over the flange.

- If the walls are wrapped while they are lying on the deck before standing them up, be sure to add a course of sheathing wrap to cover the rim joist. Remember, this course must lap under the sheathing wrap above it.

- Always wrap gable ends. This part of a house sees a lot of exposure to wind-driven water, but often is neglected when contractors assume that the sheathing wrap is meant to stop air.

- Add a second layer of sheathing wrap along inside and outside house corners, lapping at least 9 in. (an even multiple of 36-in.-wide asphalt felt) on each wall.

- Control splashback by sloping the grade around the house and keeping siding at least 8 in. above grade. At decks and stoops where splashback may be a problem, use a wide peel-and-stick flashing membrane (see "Flexible Flashing Materials," opposite page). Make sure this membrane laps under the sheathing wrap above it.

- All flashing (for windows, doors, deck ledgers, electrical fixtures, vents, pipes, and cantilevered beams) must lap under the sheathing wrap above it. Do not rely on tape to seal the flashing.

To Tape or Not

Manufacturers of plastic housewrap recommend taping all seams to block air leakage through walls. However, typical plywood and OSB sheathing are impermeable to air, so there is no need to tape all the seams.

Some tape is useful for stopping water leaks by repairing rips (particularly tears around staples) and for securing the wrap to flashing before the siding is in place. For best results, use a polypropylene tape intended for sheathing wrap or a flexible, peel-and-stick flashing. A high-quality polyurethane rubber caulk may also be used to seal plastic housewrap (see "Caulks and Sealants," page 100).

Do not patch over housewrap and rely on the stickiness of tape to seal the patch. Always lap housewrap and flashings under the piece of sheathing wrap above.

Flexible Flashing Materials

Flexible flashing — a self-adhering bituminous tape — should be used to flash all the following: exterior door sills; deck ledgers; inside and outside corners of wall sheathing; stucco shelves and parapets; below-grade concrete cracks; and wall areas subject to splashback.

Flexible flashings come in several varieties, including "peel-and-stick" products, as well as non-stick products.

Rubberized-Asphalt Flashings

Self-adhesive, rubberized asphalt flashings are made from the same materials as the eaves membranes used to prevent ice dam leaks. Typically available in rolls from 4- to 12-in. wide (but sometimes available up to 36 in. wide),

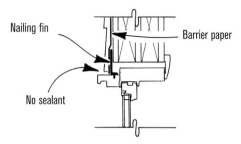

Figure 14. Flanged Window Head

Nailing fin
Barrier paper
No sealant

With flanged windows, make sure the sheathing wrap laps over the top fin. Leave a $^1/4$-in. gap between the siding and the flange, but don't caulk this gap. Water draining from above must have a place to exit.

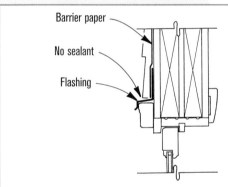

Figure 15. Unflanged Window Head

Barrier paper
No sealant
Flashing

With unflanged windows, install metal Z-flashing under the sheathing wrap and over the window head trim.

these flexible flashings can be applied directly to the sheathing, as long as the surface is warm and relatively clean.

Thickness varies from 25- to 60-mils. The thinner the material, the easier it can be folded and tucked beneath siding, but also the easier it will tear and degrade in sunlight.

Climate Cautions

- **In warm temperatures,** when rubberized asphalt is the stickiest, it is nearly impossible to reposition it once the flashing has touched the surface. Make sure to dry-fit before pulling the release paper. It is also very difficult to handle alone when it is this sticky.

- **In hot temperatures,** rubberized asphalt tends to ooze, making it messy to handle. In sunbelt areas (or wherever surface temperatures might exceed 180°F), avoid using with metal flashings; the flashings will cook and the asphalt soon dries out, usually after creating a dripping mess.

- **In cold weather,** self-adhering flashings often don't stick well. Check the manufacturer's minimum application temperature. Some stick in temperatures below 25°F, but most require surface temperatures of 40°F or greater.

Figure 16. Flashing Door Thresholds

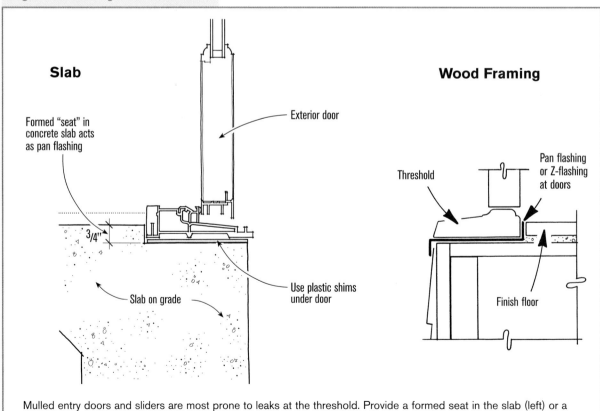

Mulled entry doors and sliders are most prone to leaks at the threshold. Provide a formed seat in the slab (left) or a metal pan flashing to keep water off the floor.

Compatibility

The solvents in rubberized asphalt will stain rolled vinyl flashing — the flexible coiled trim stock — but generally will not hurt the more rigid vinyls used for window fins and siding.

Do not use rubberized asphalt and butyl tapes together. On concrete, masonry, or OSB, rubberized-asphalt flashings may not stick well unless a primer is applied. On these surfaces, a butyl flashing works better.

Poly vs. foil. Rubberized-asphalt flashings typically come with a polyethylene or foil covering to protect them from sunlight. Poly-covered products need to be covered from sunlight within 30 to 60 days; foil-covered tapes have no exact exposure limitations but eventually will dry out and become brittle in full sunlight. Once the flashing has become brittle, any shift in surface movement will pull at the bond until either the bond fails or the membrane cracks.

Exposed applications. In permanently exposed applications, use an EPDM flashing tape instead of an inexpensive flexible flashing material. The drawback with EPDM tape is that it's expensive, as well as quite thick (about 70-mil), making it awkward to fold into small areas.

Figure 17. Flashing Deck Ledgers

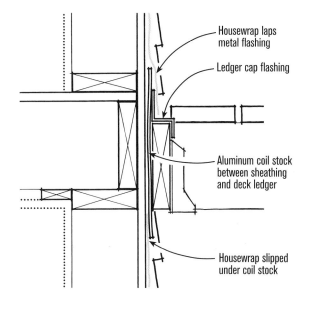

Housewrap laps metal flashing

Ledger cap flashing

Aluminum coil stock between sheathing and deck ledger

Housewrap slipped under coil stock

To properly flash a ledger, run the flashing behind the ledger to a drip-edge.

Butyl Rubber Flashings

Butyl costs about twice as much as rubberized asphalt, but yields great results: The adhesive lasts longer and sticks over a wider range of temperatures. Butyl grabs better onto rough surfaces, such as concrete and OSB, yet the bond develops slowly, allowing for easy repositioning. Also, butyl is less likely to ooze in high temperatures or to stain a finished surface.

Figure 18. Flashing Cantilever Beams

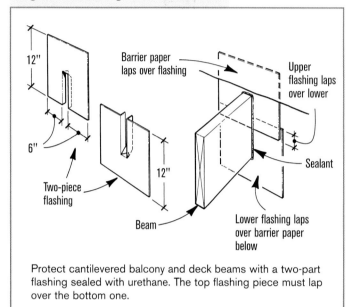

Protect cantilevered balcony and deck beams with a two-part flashing sealed with urethane. The top flashing piece must lap over the bottom one.

Figure 19. Flashing Electrical Fixtures

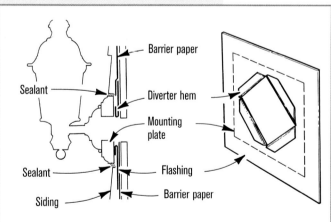

Exterior electrical boxes and fixtures can be sealed with a hemmed metal plate. Slit the sheathing wrap above the fixture and slip the plate beneath.

Like rubberized asphalt products, butyl flashings are available with either a polyethylene or foil surface. Poly-covered flashings should be covered within 30 days to protect from UV light. Foil does a good job at reflecting the UV light, but it still heats up in exposed sunlight. It will hold out longer, but when left exposed, foil-faced flashing eventually will degrade.

Compatibility. Do not use butyl flashing near any asphalt-based products. The butyl and the asphalt products will both dry out faster and loose their adhesion.

Nonstick Flashings

Not all flexible flashings are self-adhering. Some must be secured with staples or roofing nails. While generally thinner and the quickest to deteriorate in sunlight, these are often the best choice for applying beneath siding and trim in consistently cold temperatures, or when the surface is rough or dirty — factors that can diminish the bond of peel-and-stick flashings. Cover non-stick flashing as soon as possible to protect it from sunlight.

Drainage Plane

Water will always get behind siding. Wind blows in through gaps, and when the sun beats down on wet siding, it drives moisture inward. No siding material is impervious to water, and if the siding is pressed tight against plastic housewrap or applied over foam sheathing, the front of the siding tends to dry while the back stays wet. This stresses all types of siding: It cups boards, curls shingles, accelerates stucco cracks, and weakens mortar bonds in brick veneer. With all siding, an air space behind the siding ($1/4$- to $3/8$-in. is enough) will allow water to drain and the backside of the siding to dry.

Well-Drained Wall Systems

Different sidings call for different drainage details. Typical details for well-draining walls are shown for different types of siding:

Board siding, **Figure 37**, page 38;

Shake and shingle siding, **Figure 41**, page 44;

Vinyl siding, **Figure 51**, page 53;

Stucco, **Figure 66**, page 69.

In each case, an air space must be created behind the siding and an exit provided for water to drain out.

Flashing Details

- Never rely on the stickiness of peel-and-stick flashings for sealing; the bond is unlikely to last over the lifespan of the house.

- Always lap flashings under the sheathing wrap above.

Flashing Windows

Do not X-cut sheathing wrap at openings. Instead, I-cut the sheathing wrap, running the knife horizontally along the rough opening at the head and sill, then slitting vertically in the center of the opening (**Figure 10**, page 9). This way, the window flange can be slipped under the sheathing wrap when installing the window.

Sill details: Install a beveled cant strip or narrow dam strip to the rough opening sill, then wrap the sill with sheathing wrap or a flexible flashing membrane (**Figure 11**, page 10). Make sure this membrane drapes over the sheathing wrap below.

All sheathing wrap must be integrated with flashing materials. It's not enough to wrap a house, and then to simply X-cut the openings and fold the flaps inside. Follow the guidelines in **Figure 10** (page 9) when installing any sheathing wrap.

Figure 20. Flashing Penetrations

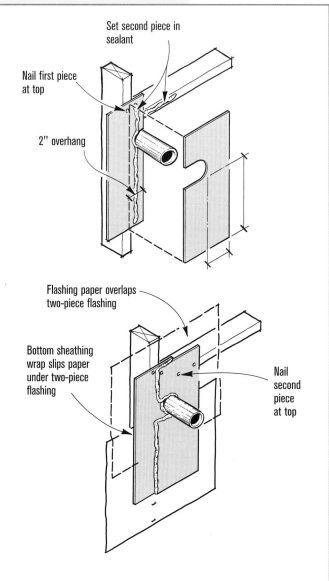

Set second piece in sealant

Nail first piece at top

2" overhang

Flashing paper overlaps two-piece flashing

Bottom sheathing wrap slips paper under two-piece flashing

Nail second piece at top

To seal around wall penetrations, use a two-piece metal plate bedded in urethane sealant. Sheathing wrap above the metal plate should lap over the plate while sheathing wrap below it should be slipped beneath.

Window and Door Splines

Water will leak through the gap where the siding butts the casing. Even if this joint is caulked, the sealant won't last as long as the paint job, and water will eventually work itself inside. Windows and doors should be flashed with felt paper or flexible flashing splines (**Figure 12**, page 11). The splines should be installed after the sill flashing, and the sheathing wrap should go on afterwards or be slit so it laps over the splines.

Flanged window heads do not need additional flashing. The nailing fin will do a good job sealing the head if it can be tucked beneath the sheathing wrap when the window is installed (**Figure 14**, page 13). Leave a $1/4$-in. gap between the siding and the window along the head, but do not caulk this gap. Otherwise, water that runs behind the siding from above won't have a place to drain.

If the flange cannot be tucked under the sheathing wrap when the window is installed, slit the wrap and add a head flashing, as shown in **Figure 13**, page 12.

Unflanged windows will need an additional metal Z-flashing above the head casing or brick mold, as shown in

Figure 15, page 13. Make sure this Z-flashing laps underneath the sheathing wrap.

Mulled windows and window walls must have a continuous head flashing; the manufacturer's mullion cover will not prevent water from running between the window units from above.

Round-top windows should be flashed with a peel-and-stick flexible flashing. Slit the sheathing wrap and slip it underneath, letting it drape over the window top. Then cut the flashing to conform to the nailing fin. Rely on proper lapping of the flashing, not on caulk.

Flashing Doors

Water that gets past siding and trim around doors can run along the floor, ruining finish flooring. This is a particular problem where splashback from dripping eaves and overhangs soaks the door. Over wood floors, door thresholds should be flashed with a metal pan or Z-flashing. Slabs should be formed with a "seat" to hold the threshold (**Figure 16**, page 14).

Flashing Ledgers and Beams

Ledger flashing needs to be more than a Z-flashing running along the top edge of the ledger board. Use metal coil stock behind the ledger, as shown in **Figure 17**, page 15. Make sure the coil stock slips under the sheathing wrap above the ledger, and drapes over the sheathing wrap below the ledger.

Alternatively, build a deck completely free-standing from the wall, or insert spacers between the ledger board and the wall, so it stands out and allows water to drain freely.

Cantilevered deck or balcony joists that project through the wall framing are trouble spots. Flash with a two-piece flashing membrane, as shown in **Figure 18**, page 16.

Flashing Wall Penetrations

Electrical fixtures. Install electrical boxes and lighting fixtures on a hemmed metal flashing plate, as shown in **Figure 19**, page 16. Do not tape the plate over the sheathing wrap; slit the sheathing wrap and tuck it beneath.

Mechanical penetrations. Gas line, conduit, water spigots, and other small

Figure 21. Kickout Flashing

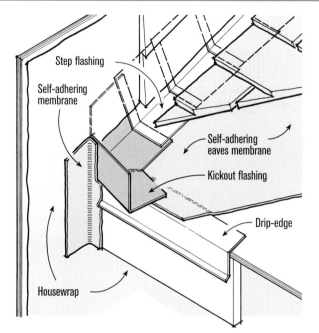

Step flashing

Self-adhering membrane

Self-adhering eaves membrane

Kickout flashing

Drip-edge

Housewrap

To prevent water from dumping behind the siding at the end of a roof intersection, bend a small "kickout" from metal flashing to divert water running down the roof away from the siding.

penetrations should be flashed with a two-piece metal flashing plate (**Figure 20**, page 18). Seal the two plates with a "low modulus" urethane caulk (see "Caulks and Sealants," page 100).

Sidewall Flashing

Because of the volume of water that can pour down a sloped roof, one of the most critical flashing details occurs where a roof intersects a sidewall. The roof should be flashed with a step flashing. Where the roof terminates, install a kick-out to deflect water away from the siding (**Figure 21**).

Though not always possible in the schedule, it's best to install a full 36-in. piece of rubberized asphalt flashing on the wall before the subfascia and trim boards are nailed in place, and then come back to install the kickout.

Siding Nails

Use only galvanized or stainless-steel nails for exterior siding and trim. Stainless-steel nails will resist corrosion the longest, but they are very expensive. Double hot-dipped galvanized nails are the next best choice. High-tensile aluminum nails can be used for a low-budget job.

Galvanized Nail Coatings

Galvanized coatings vary widely. The following coating types are available (in order from best to worst):

Hot-dipped zinc-coated nails offer the best protection among the galvanized nails. Because nails are submerged in molten zinc, they are coated uniformly and the high heat causes the zinc and steel to fuse. Nails can be double-dipped for heavier plating. True hot-dipped nails are hard to distinguish from hot-galvanized nails; for verification, look for ASTM-153, the standard for hot-dipped galvanized hardware.

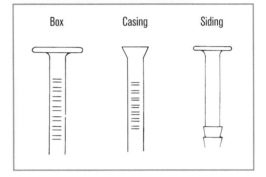

Figure 22. Exterior Nail Types

Box   Casing   Siding

Electroplated nails work best in nail guns. The nails are immersed in an electrolytic solution that deposits a thin film of zinc on them when an electric current is run through the solution. Because the coating is thin, it oxidizes in harsh exposures to salt air and pollution.

Mechanically plated nails are rotated when cold in a barrel of zinc dust. Glass beads hammer the zinc onto the nail, and then the nails are immersed in a chromate solution, which gives them a gold or greenish color. This process leaves threaded nails clean, but the coating is thin.

Figure 23. Extractive Bleeding

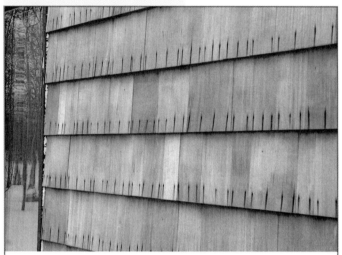

Bleeding is caused by excessive moisture in siding, which reacts to the iron in nails — even when the nail is intact. To prevent bleeding, keep siding dry before installation and seal it soon afterwards.

Hot-galvanized nails are the least effective. The nails are rotated in a barrel in a furnace to melt the zinc. They may not be evenly coated and threads may fill up.

Selecting Galvanized Nails

For best results, choose nails with an appropriate head, shank, and point, as shown in **Figure 24**.

Extractive Bleeding

Natural-finished siding may stain around nails, as shown in **Figure 23**. Even painted and stained siding may become discolored. This staining can occur even when the galvanized coating of the nail is intact, and with stainless-steel and aluminum nails. The staining is caused when a high moisture content in wood dissolves the wood's naturally occurring extractives — pigments, tannins, oils, and resins. These extractives then react with the iron in the nail to form a blue-black stain around the nail head. A poor quality nail makes the problem worse because gaps in the galvanizing expose the extractives to unprotected iron.

To prevent extractive bleeding, condition the siding and protect it from water before installation (see "Conditioning Siding," page 38). Back-prime the siding to help seal extractives in the wood, and install the siding on a rain screen to promote drying. Seal or paint the wood when it is dry and maintain the finish to keep wood dry over time (see "Finishes," page 103).

Figure 24. Selecting Siding Nails

For Cedar, Redwood, and Other Premium Board Sidings

Features	Advantages
High-Grade Steel	Under the galvanized coating, high-carbon steel minimizes bending, even with thin-shank nails.
Shank	A ring-shank nail provides 50% to 100% greater holding power than a smooth-shank nail. Recommended penetration is $1\frac{1}{2}$ in. into the solid wood stud. A thin-shank nail will reduce wood splits that occur with standard-thickness siding nails.
Point	A blunt point punches its way though siding material rather than wedging though wood fibers, reducing the chance of splits.
Head Size	A small head helps to make the nail unobtrusive on fine wood siding. For painted sidings, choose a checker-head nail, which greatly increases paint adhesion.

For Hardboard, Plywood, and Fiber-Cement Siding

Features	Advantages
High-Grade Steel	Under the galvanized coating, high-carbon steel minimizes bending when the nail is driven through two laps of siding.
Threaded Shank	A ring or a spiral shank provides much better holding power and reducing nail "pop-outs."
Head Size	Use a minimum $1/4$-in.-diameter head for blind nails; use a larger roofing nail head for face nailing. A larger, flat head will help prevent the head from breaking through the surface.

For Vinyl Siding

Features	Advantages
High-Grade Steel	Drives much better than aluminum nails.
Threaded Shank	Spiral shanks hold much better than smooth shanks.
Head Size	The large head allows the siding to hang properly without slipping though the expansion slot.

For long-lasting results, all exterior siding and trim nails should be double hot-dipped galvanized, or Type 304 or 316 stainless steel.

Wood Trim

Exterior trim serves both a functional and an aesthetic purpose. Its primary function is to divert water away from vulnerable areas of walls, such as roof intersections, window and door openings, and wall corners — all places where wind-driven rain can seep into the wall cavity (**Figure 25**). Aesthetically, exterior trim provides a visual transition between wall surfaces and openings, edges, and corners.

Wood Selection

Rot-resistant woods include redwood, red cedar, Alaskan yellow cedar, and Port Orford cedar, all of which may last a century or more without protection. These woods are easy to work with and they take paint well, but they are soft and dent easily.

Depending on the region of the country, other durable woods may be available. These include high-quality cypress, white oak, and locust. These species offer nearly the same rot resistance as redwood but are much stronger.

Moderately rot-resistant woods include eastern white pine, southern longleaf pine, larch, and swamp oak. These woods may last for many years if they are installed properly and are well-protected with exterior finish.

Slightly resistant or nonresistant woods include alder, poplar, cottonwood, hemlock, the spruces, the maples, red oak, and all other pines and true firs. Do not use these species for exterior trim unless it can be guaranteed that no water ever reaches the raw wood.

Cull Out Defects

Regardless of species, avoid any board containing a large percentage of

Figure 25. Durable Exterior Trim

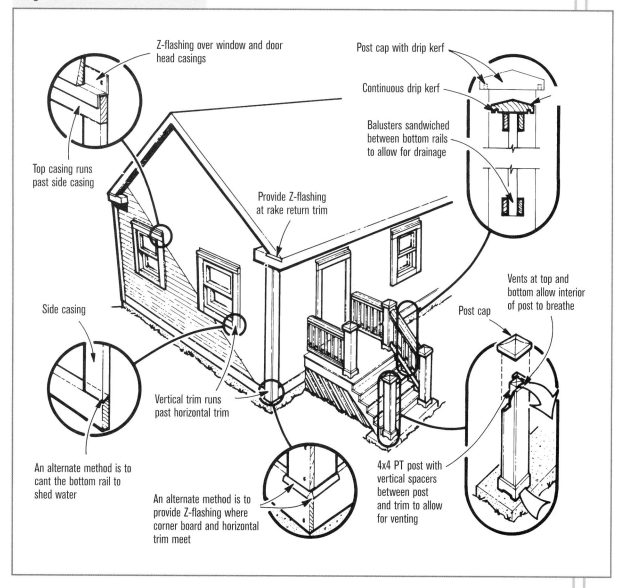

Z-flashing over window and door head casings

Post cap with drip kerf

Continuous drip kerf

Balusters sandwiched between bottom rails to allow for drainage

Top casing runs past side casing

Provide Z-flashing at rake return trim

Side casing

Vents at top and bottom allow interior of post to breathe

Post cap

Vertical trim runs past horizontal trim

An alternate method is to cant the bottom rail to shed water

An alternate method is to provide Z-flashing where corner board and horizontal trim meet

4x4 PT post with vertical spacers between post and trim to allow for venting

Figure 26. Exterior Casings Over Flanged Windows

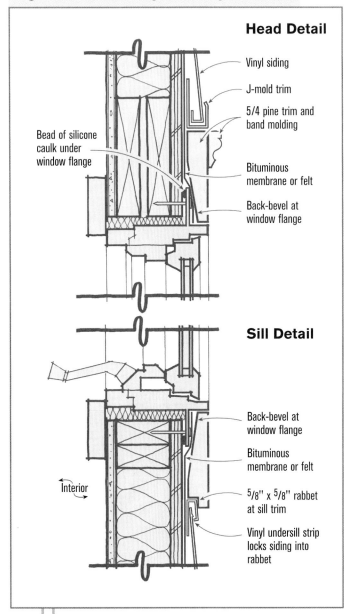

Head Detail

Vinyl siding

J-mold trim

5/4 pine trim and band molding

Bead of silicone caulk under window flange

Bituminous membrane or felt

Back-bevel at window flange

Sill Detail

Back-bevel at window flange

Bituminous membrane or felt

$^5/_8$" x $^5/_8$" rabbet at sill trim

Interior

Vinyl undersill strip locks siding into rabbet

sapwood, as sapwood is less durable than heartwood. Also avoid boards with splits, surface cracks, or loose knots. These defects will always get worse with exposure to the elements, and provide entry for bugs and fungi.

Design Principles of Exterior Woodwork

Exterior joints should be designed to shed water (**Figure 25**, page 25). Trapped water will cause excessive wood movement and splitting, and eventually will invite rot, bugs, and fungal infestations.

Avoid Miter Joints

Only profiled moldings should be mitered; all other trim boards should have lap joints. Miter joints inevitably open as the wood shrinks, exposing the end grain of both boards to the weather.

While all trim stock should be dry (less than 12% MC at installation), this is especially important for profiled moldings to keep miters tight. Pre-prime all sides to help keep the wood dry.

Seal and Flash Edges

To keep joints dry, first make them as tight as possible:

- Make sure that adjoining surfaces meet uniformly at all points; no amount of glue or fasteners can compensate for a sloppy joint.

- Seal all joints that are likely to absorb water. Horizontal joints are the most vulnerable. Apply a coat of latex paint or a wax-based sealant such as Thompson's Water Seal® before the pieces are assembled.

Second, use metal flashing to help water find a path away from horizontal trim pieces.

Canted Surfaces and Drip Edges

Railings, thresholds, and other flat surfaces can be made to shed water by bowing or sloping top surfaces, and by sawing or routing a drip groove along their undersides. Build ventilation channels around posts and columns, that will allow built-up pieces to dry.

Exterior Casing

Always apply Z-flashing over the head casing, and lap the head casing over

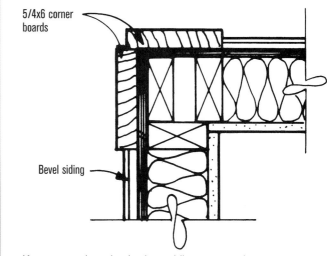

Figure 27. Corner Reveal

5/4x6 corner boards

Bevel siding

Keep corner boards plumb so siding cuts can be cut square. A reveal at the outside corner will help compensate for out-of-plumb walls.

the side casings. Either extend side casings past the apron or cant at the bottom on a sloped sill (**Figure 25**, page 25). Keep sills as narrow as possible to limit exposure.

To keep casings flat and joints aligned, back-bevel casing stock to fit over window flanges (**Figure 26**). Rabbet the bottom edge of window aprons to divert water from the joint between the window trim and siding.

Figure 28. Corner Treatments

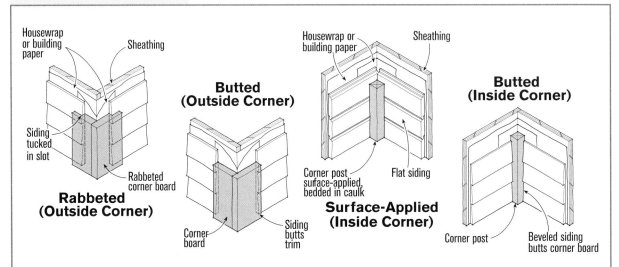

A rabbeted corner board will work best to protect siding at outside corners. This detail is critical for vulnerable siding such as hardboard. On flat siding profiles, an inside corner post bedded in caulk can overlay the siding, but beveled siding should butt.

Corner Boards

All corners should be double-flashed with sheathing wrap or flexible flashing (see **Figure 10**, page 9).

Outside Corners

Mitered outside corners should be avoided unless metal corner flashing is used (see **Figure 65**, page 67). The best way to handle outside corners with most sidings is with corner boards (**Figure 28**). Rabbeted edges will work the best to protect the joint between the corner board and the siding. Do not miter or caulk either side of the corner boards. The caulk will fail faster than the paint job and could trap water. Rely on careful corner flashing instead.

Tall walls may not always be framed perfectly plumb. To compensate (so siding cut can be level and square), build in a reveal, which will help to hide slight discrepancies (**Figure 27,** page 27).

Figure 29. Simple Wood Cornices

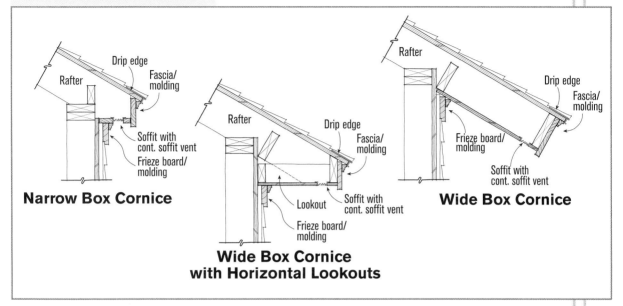

Narrow Box Cornice — Drip edge, Rafter, Fascia/molding, Soffit with cont. soffit vent, Frieze board/molding

Wide Box Cornice with Horizontal Lookouts — Rafter, Drip edge, Fascia/molding, Lookout, Soffit with cont. soffit vent, Frieze board/molding

Wide Box Cornice — Rafter, Drip edge, Fascia/molding, Frieze board/molding, Soffit with cont. soffit vent

Inside Corners

Inside corners are best handled with a square corner post (**Figure 28**).

Wood Cornices

A wide cornice is one of the best ways to protect walls from water. Conversely, walls without overhangs will always leak. Rake overhangs are just as important as eaves overhangs. Remember, water doesn't flow just downhill; it is driven in all directions by the wind, and a rake overhang will protect the vulnerable roof-to-gable intersection.

A cornice includes frieze board, soffit, and fascia. Several different width overhangs are shown in **Figure 29**. With an elaborate cornice over brick veneer, frame-in short pony walls to support the soffit and frieze (**Figure 30**).

Eaves Crown

Crown molding is a common detail on traditional Colonial, Georgian, and Federal period houses. The most difficult detail is at the eaves-rake transition. There are only two ways to turn the corner with the crown and match the profile: Either cut one piece of trim for the eaves and one piece for the rake (called matched profiles) or return the crown horizontally and terminate the rake crown on top of the cornice return (**Figure 31**).

Gable-End Transitions

Just as a fascia is protected by the roof's drip-edge, other horizontal runs, such as head casing and skirt boards, should be protected by a drip-cap and Z-flashing. This is especially important on transition boards, such as the joint between gable siding and the wall below (**Figure 32**).

Tudor Trim Details

The key to leak-free details in a traditional Tudor exterior is to install "build-out boards" behind the 1x6 cedar trim (**Figure 33**).

Vertical and Angled Trim

Install vertical and angled trim over 4-in.-wide plywood "build-out" boards. The narrower build-out board allows the scratch and brown coats of stucco to be troweled in behind the 1x6 (see "Three-Coat Stucco," page 74). Then, run the finish coat tight to the edge of the overlapping 1x6 trim board. Angled board details are problematic since they channel water towards the interior of the wall. Always flash behind diagonal boards with flexible flashing membranes.

Figure 30. Traditional Cornice with Brick Veneer

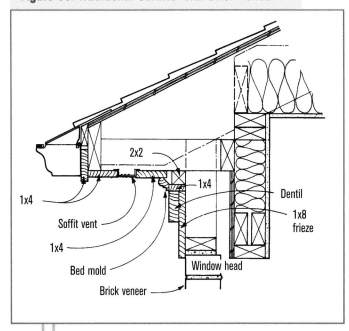

2x2

1x4

1x4

Dentil

1x8 frieze

Soffit vent

1x4

Bed mold

Window head

Brick veneer

Figure 31. Crown Return

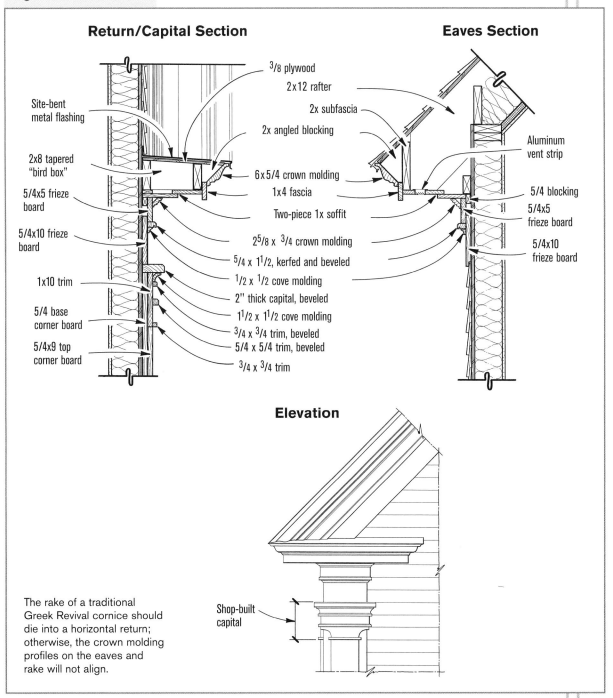

Return/Capital Section

3/8 plywood

2x12 rafter

2x subfascia

2x angled blocking

Site-bent metal flashing

2x8 tapered "bird box"

5/4x5 frieze board

5/4x10 frieze board

1x10 trim

5/4 base corner board

5/4x9 top corner board

6 x 5/4 crown molding

1x4 fascia

Two-piece 1x soffit

$2^{5}/_{8}$ x $^{3}/_{4}$ crown molding

$^{5}/_{4}$ x $1^{1}/_{2}$, kerfed and beveled

$^{1}/_{2}$ x $^{1}/_{2}$ cove molding

2" thick capital, beveled

$1^{1}/_{2}$ x $1^{1}/_{2}$ cove molding

$^{3}/_{4}$ x $^{3}/_{4}$ trim, beveled

5/4 x 5/4 trim, beveled

$^{3}/_{4}$ x $^{3}/_{4}$ trim

Eaves Section

Aluminum vent strip

5/4 blocking

5/4x5 frieze board

5/4x10 frieze board

Elevation

Shop-built capital

The rake of a traditional Greek Revival cornice should die into a horizontal return; otherwise, the crown molding profiles on the eaves and rake will not align.

Figure 32. Siding Transition

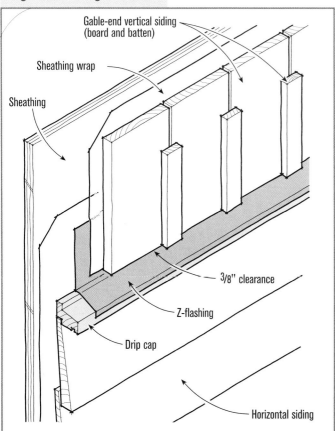

Gable-end vertical siding
(board and batten)

Sheathing wrap

Sheathing

3/8" clearance

Z-flashing

Drip cap

Horizontal siding

To divert water away from horizontal siding when vertical siding is used on gable ends, install a transition board with a drip-cap and Z-flashing.

Horizontal Trim

Unlike vertical trim, horizontal trim is held flush with the upper edges of the build-out board. Run Z-flashing continuously across the tops of horizontal boards, making sure to lap sheathing wrap over the Z-flashing so water drains down and out.

Seal Trim Before Installation

Tudor trim boards should be sealed with paint or stain on all sides (including field cuts) before installation.

Figure 33. Tudor Trim Details

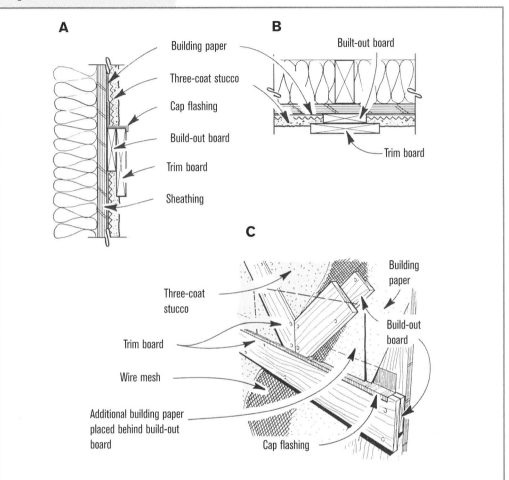

A

- Building paper
- Three-coat stucco
- Cap flashing
- Build-out board
- Trim board
- Sheathing

B

- Built-out board
- Trim board

C

- Three-coat stucco
- Building paper
- Trim board
- Build-out board
- Wire mesh
- Additional building paper placed behind build-out board
- Cap flashing

Tudor trim set in stucco must be carefully flashed. Avoid diagonal trim if possible; the diagonals channel water down. If diagonals can't be avoided, flash the wall with peel-and-stick flashing membrane where the boards end, and provide a metal Z-flashing on horizontal trim pieces.

Board Siding

Siding Grades

Problems occur with siding grades that are unsuitable for the job. To avoid problems, use select grades. Lumberyards may use other terms for their siding grades, but there's little chance of knowing what will be delivered or how it will perform. Ask for equivalents to the standard grades established by industry trade associations shown in **Figure 34**. Cheap or ungraded siding usually warps, shrinks, splits, and otherwise deteriorates far quicker than premium-grade material.

Moisture Content

Nearly all wood siding shrinks somewhat after installation. If the wood is too wet when installed, excessive shrinkage can lead to splitting, warping, cupping, or paint checking. Problems can be minimized by specifying "S-Dry" material, which contains no more than 19% moisture, or by using premium-grade materials.

MC on Delivery

Unseasoned or green wood has a moisture content (MC) of more than 19%. Dry wood has a maximum moisture content of 15% or 19% depending upon grade. Premium grades are dried to MC 15, meaning that the wood has

Figure 35. Storing Siding On Site

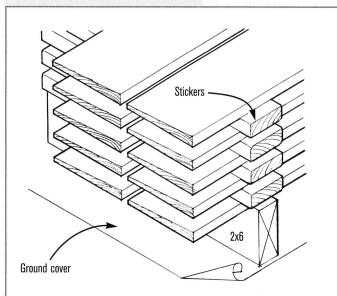

It's best to get any wood siding at least a week early and store it at the job site to let it adjust to the site's humidity. Keep siding out of weather in the driest space available. Break apart bundles and restack the material on evenly spaced, vertically aligned stickers to allow air to circulate freely.

Figure 34. Wood Siding Grades

Product	Grade	Description	Moisture Content
Standard Clear Grades — Western Red Cedar			
Bevel Siding	Clear VG (vertical grain)	Free of knots and imperfections; for use where the highest quality appearance is desired.	MC-15 (15% or less — most pieces 12% or less)
	A Grade	Includes some mixed grain and minor growth characteristics.	
	B Grade	Includes mixed grain, limited characteristics and occasional cutouts in longer pieces.	
	Rustic	Similar to A grade, but graded from sawn face.	
	C Grade	Admits larger and more numerous than A or B grades.	
Boards (Finish, Trim)	Clear	Finest appearance with clear face, few minor characteristics.	MC-15 (15% or less — most pieces 12% or less)
	A Grade	Recommended for fine appearance. May include minor imperfections or growth characteristics.	
	B Grade	Permits larger and more characteristics, but may have short lengths of fine appearance.	
Standard Knotty Grades — Western Red Cedar			
Bevel Siding, Boards, Channel, T&G, etc.	Select Knotty Quality Knotty	For fine knotty appearance. Permits more pronounced characteristics and has occasional cutouts in longer pieces.	19% or less
	Select Merchantable Construction	Has fine appearance and includes knots and minor markings. Limited characteristics allowed to assure high degree of serviceability.	Unseasoned
	Standard	Allows more characteristics than construction.	
Standard Softwood Grades (all species except redwood)			
All board patterns	C select	Mixed grain, a few small knots allowed. For uses where a fine finished appearance is desired.	MC-15 (15% or less — most pieces 12% or less)
	D select	Mixed grain, slightly larger knots than allowed in C Select.	
All board patterns	#2 common	Has fine appearance and includes knots and minor markings.	19% or less
	#3 common	Limited characteristics allowed to assure high degree of serviceability.	
	#4 common	Allows more characteristics than #3. Used chiefly for serviceability rather than appearance.	

Note: These grades apply to all lumber graded under the rules of Western Wood Products Assoc. (WWPA), West Coast Lumber Inspection Bureau (WCLIB), or National Lumber Grades Authority (NLGA) of Canada. The term "characteristics" refers to knots, wane, pitch pockets, irregular grain, etc.

Figure 36. Board Siding Patterns

Siding Patterns	Nominal Sizes (thickness and width)	Nailing (Do not nail where siding pieces overlay)	
		6 in. and narrower	**8 in. and wider**
Bevel or Bungalow Bungalow (Colonial) is slightly thicker than Bevel. Either can be used with the smooth or rough-faced surface exposed. Patterns provide a traditional-style appearance. Horizontal applications only. 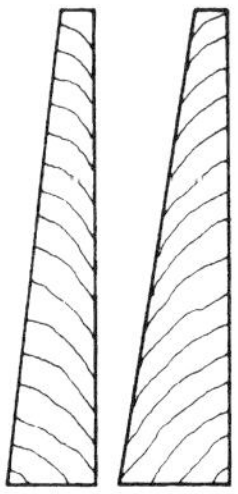	1/2 x 4 1/2 x 5 1/2 x 6 5/8 x 8 5/8 x 10 3/4 x 6 3/4 x 8 3/4 x 10	Recommend 1" overlap. One siding nail or box nail per bearing, just above the 1" overlap.  Plain	Recommend 1" overlap. One siding nail or box nail per bearing, just above the 1" overlap. 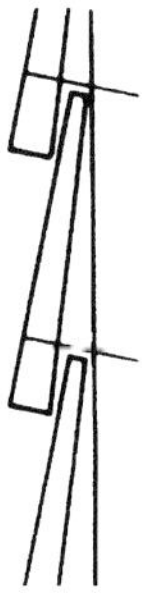 Plain
Tongue & Groove T&G siding is available in a variety of patterns. Vertical or horizontal applications. Install horizontal T&G with the tongues up so the joint will drain. 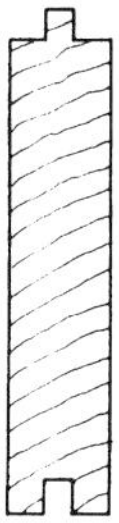	1 x 4 1 x 6 1 x 8 1 x 10 Available with 1/4", 3/8", or 7/16" tongues. For wider widths, specify the longer tongue.	Use one casing nail per bearing to blind nail. 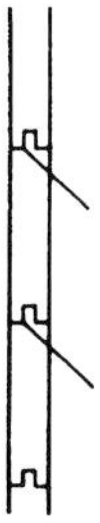 Plain	Use two siding nails or box nails 3" to 4" apart to face nail. 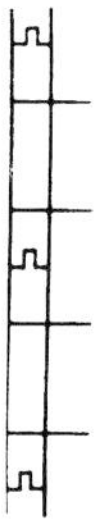 Plain

Figure 36. Board Siding Patterns, continued

Siding Patterns	Nominal Sizes (thickness and width)	Nailing (Do not nail where siding pieces overlay)	
		6 in. and narrower	8 in. and wider
Channel Rustic Channel Rustic has 1/2" overlap and a 1" to 11/4" channel when installed. The profile allows for maximum dimensional change without harming appearance. Available smooth, rough or saw-textured. Horizontal or vertical applications.	3/4 x 6 3/4 x 8 3/4 x 10	Use one siding nail or box nail to face nail once per bearing, 1" up from bottom edge.	Use two siding nails or box nails 3" to 4" apart per bearing.
Board-and-Batten Boards are surfaced smooth, rough or saw-textured. Rustic ranch-style appearance. Requires horizontal nailers. Vertical applications only.	(4/4) 1 x 2 1 x 4 1 x 6 1 x 8 1 x 10 1 x 12 (5/4) 11/4 x 6 11/4 x 8 11/4 x 10 11/4 x 12	Recommend 1/2" overlap. One siding or box nail per bearing. 1/2" Board-and-Batten	Increase overlap proportionately. Use two siding nails or box nails, 3" to 4" apart. Board-and-Batten Board-on-Board

15% moisture content or less (and that 85% of the pieces are dried to 12% or less). Dry siding will acclimate more quickly to its final surroundings and will have less dimensional change, before or after installation, than unseasoned or green siding.

MC at Installation

Condition all board siding. Moisture content will vary from piece to piece, but the material should average about 12% MC at the time of installation (individual pieces ranging from 9% to 14%). In dry southwestern states, siding should average 9% MC.

Conditioning Siding

Wood siding picks up and loses moisture in transit and storage, so it is important to allow it to acclimate to the site before installation (**Figure 35**, page 34):

- "Splinter" bundles by breaking them up and stacking them with stickers (spacers between every layer).

- If stacked over the ground or concrete, lay poly down first, and then use 2x6s to elevate the first layer.

- Stack siding in a dry area where plenty of air can flow through the stack, and protect it from weather.

- Store on site 7 to 10 days before installation. Extend drying period to 30 days for unseasoned siding or during very humid seasons.

Board Siding Patterns

Pattern is more than just an aesthetic choice. Certain patterns respond better than others to climate changes (**Figure 36,** pages 36-37).

Pattern Width

Narrow patterns perform best because there is less movement from wet to dry periods and with seasonal climate changes.

Figure 37. Drainage Plane for Board Siding

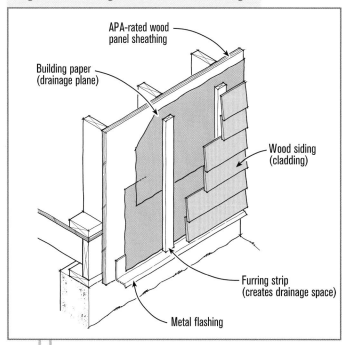

APA-rated wood panel sheathing

Building paper (drainage plane)

Wood siding (cladding)

Furring strip (creates drainage space)

Metal flashing

Figure 38. Drainage Plane Details

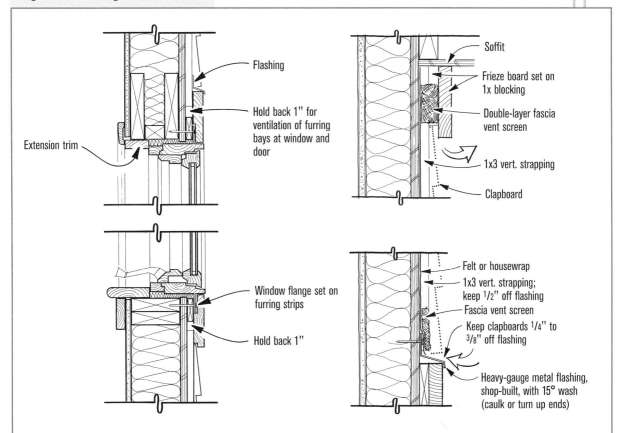

Flashing

Hold back 1" for ventilation of furring bays at window and door

Extension trim

Soffit

Frieze board set on 1x blocking

Double-layer fascia vent screen

1x3 vert. strapping

Clapboard

Window flange set on furring strips

Hold back 1"

Felt or housewrap

1x3 vert. strapping; keep 1/2" off flashing

Fascia vent screen

Keep clapboards 1/4" to 3/8" off flashing

Heavy-gauge metal flashing, shop-built, with 15° wash (caulk or turn up ends)

If siding is installed on battens, window and door jambs must be extended (left), and the gap created by the strapping should be screened at the top and the bottom (right) to keep out insects.

Wide patterns will cover an area faster, thus reducing labor costs, but any savings may be offset by callbacks due to warping, cupping, or checking. Avoid patterns over 8 in. in width.

Drainage Plane

The easiest way to create a drainage plane is to use a self-draining rainscreen mat, such as Home Slicker® (Benjamin Obdyke; 800/346-7655; www.obdyke.com). This material is thin enough that windows, doors, and

Figure 39. Horizontal Siding Details

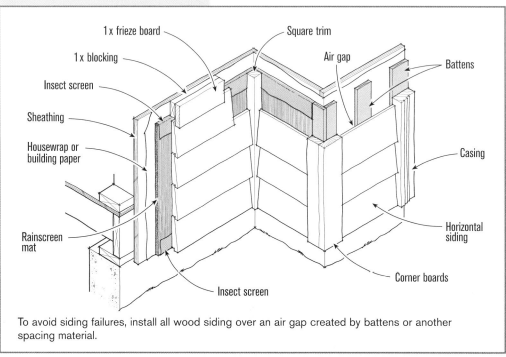

1x frieze board
Square trim
1x blocking
Air gap
Insect screen
Battens
Sheathing
Housewrap or building paper
Casing
Rainscreen mat
Horizontal siding
Insect screen
Corner boards

To avoid siding failures, install all wood siding over an air gap created by battens or another spacing material.

corners don't need to be packed out when used with 5/4 trim stock.

Also, siding may be installed over vertical battens spaced 16- to 24-in. apart to create the air space (**Figure 37**, page 38). In this case, door and window jambs must be extended to accommodate the added thickness, and a vent strip or screen should also be included over weep channels to keep out insects (**Figure 38**, page 39).

Trim for Board Siding

For information about detailing exterior wood trim for board siding, see "Wood Trim," pages 24-33.

Installing Horizontal Siding

Bevel siding is the most forgiving pattern because it's designed to shed water, and cross-grain shrinkage will not expose the wall beneath. See **Figure 39** for horizontal installation details.

Problems can develop from too much overlap. Buy bevel siding only $3/4$- to 1-in. wider than the desired reveal. A large overlap may require double-nailing (which can cause splitting) or nailing through the thinnest part of the board (which can lead to excessive cupping).

Installing Vertical Siding

Installing vertical siding over battens to create a rainscreen can be problematic. Battens must be run horizontally to hold the siding boards, but then the channels won't drain. Install vertical siding over a self-draining rainscreen backing material. See **Figure 40**, for vertical installation details.

Vertical T&G siding is more weatherproof than board-and-batten or edged-butted boards. However, all vertical siding is more prone to leaks than most horizontal board siding. Take extra care with sheathing wrap and flashing behind all vertical siding.

Extend the lower ends of vertical siding below the sheathing to allow water to drain. To prevent wicking and water staining, seal the bottom end-grain of vertical siding with water repellent.

Diagonal Board Siding

Diagonal siding is not recommended. The joints in diagonal siding act like gutters, collecting and channeling water downward at an angle against the sides of windows, doorways, corner boards, and any horizontal or vertical piece that stands in its path. Without very careful flashing and drainage plane preparation, the runoff will gush into the building at these points.

Nailing Checklist

Proper nailing is essential to the performance of any wood siding.

- Always use non-corrosive fasteners (see "Siding Nails," page 21).

- Drive siding nails flush with the surface of the siding. Nails that are set and filled are prone to popping with any movement or shrinkage in the wall framing, and may promote cupping and splitting. However, casing nails used to fasten exterior trim should be set and filled (see "Filling Nail Holes," page 109).

- Nails should penetrate at least 1- to $1^1/2$-in. into studs or blocking.

Figure 40. Vertical Siding Details

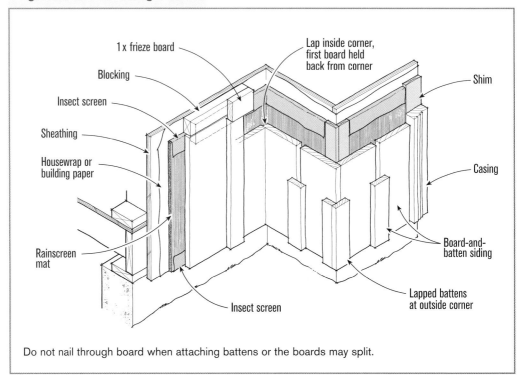

1x frieze board

Blocking

Insect screen

Sheathing

Housewrap or building paper

Rainscreen mat

Insect screen

Lap inside corner, first board held back from corner

Shim

Casing

Board-and-batten siding

Lapped battens at outside corner

Do not nail through board when attaching battens or the boards may split.

- Ring-shank or spiral-shank siding nails are recommended for increased holding power (**Figure 24**, page 23).

- Never double-nail solid wood siding materials. If the siding is pinned along both edges, it is likely to split. See **Figure 36**, pages 36-37 for proper nailing configurations for different siding patterns.

Board Siding Over Foam

Siding applied directly over rigid insulated sheathing has a history of failures. Since the foil behind the siding is impermeable, moisture collects on the back of the siding. The back of the siding absorbs moisture at a faster rate than the finished front side, causing boards to cup inwards. That same moisture will be drawn through the siding when the sun comes out, causing the finish to blister. This cycle of wetting and drying is accelerated because the insulation prevents the wall framing from absorbing any of the heat generated by exposure to direct sun.

To prevent siding problems over foam:

- **Rainscreen.** Install siding over furring strips or rainscreen backer, creating a drainage plain or "rain screen" (see "Drainage Plane for Shakes and Shingles", page 44). The resulting air space allows both heat and moisture to dissipate.

- **Back-prime.** All wood siding should always be back-primed (on natural finish material, use a clear water-repellent preservative; see "Finishes," page 103). This will slow the cycle of wetting and drying. Field-cut ends should also be coated with stain or preservative.

- **Foil caution.** Foil-faced foam is a moisture barrier, so it creates a wrong-side vapor barrier. Foam should be used only with a continuous-film vapor retarder on the inside wall to keep condensation out of the wall cavity.

Wood Shingles and Shakes

Shingle and Shake Grades

Wood shingles and shakes are made from redwood, western red cedar, northern white cedar, and cypress.

Figure 41. Drainage Plane for Shingle Siding

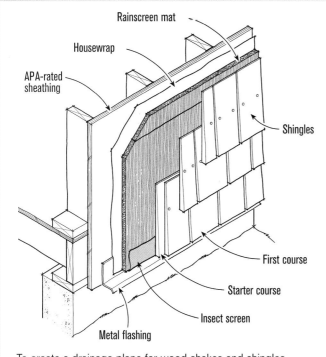

To create a drainage plane for wood shakes and shingles, install the siding over a drainage mat that will provide a channel to allow water down and out.

Most shingles are sawn smooth on both faces. Shakes are thicker and have at least one split surface, which leaves a rough texture.

Shingle and shake grades for sidewalls are largely the same as those used for roofs. The exception is machine-grooved shakes (also called "rebutted/ regrooved shingles"). These are sawn into 16-, 18-, and 24-in. lengths (butts measuring .4 in., .45 in., and .5 in., respectively) with parallel edges, and the face is grooved with striations. Machine-grooved shakes should be double-coursed (see "Double Coursing" page 47).

Drainage Plane for Shakes and Shingles

The most practical way to create a drainage plane for shingle and shake siding is with a self-draining rainscreen mat (**Figure 41**).

Figure 42. Inside and Outside Corners

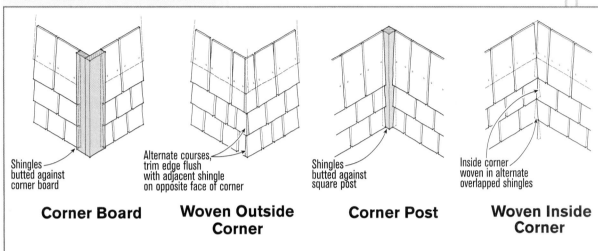

Shingles butted against corner board

Alternate courses, trim edge flush with adjacent shingle on opposite face of corner

Shingles butted against square post

Inside corner woven in alternate overlapped shingles

Corner Board

Woven Outside Corner

Corner Post

Woven Inside Corner

A woven corner, typically accomplished with a block plane, is made by alternately lapping a shingle piece on each course. Inside corners may also be woven, but the easiest and cleanest treatment is to butt shingles against a 1- to 2-in.-square post.

If the wall is furred out, horizontal battens will block drainage unless they are installed over opposing vertical battens (spaced 16- to 24-in. o.c.), creating a grid of strapping. Space horizontal battens the length of the shingle, and space vertical battens 16- to 24-in. o.c. With double thickness 1x battens, pack out windows, doors, and corners with 2x material.

Prior to installing strapping or a rainscreen mat, wrap and flash wall sheathing (see "Sheathing Wrap and Flashing," page 8).

Trim for Shingles and Shakes

Like other wood and wood-based sidings, most exterior trim for shingles and shakes can be handled with wood. For information about detailing exterior wood trim, see "Wood Trim," page 24.

Shingle and Shake Corner Treatments

Corner boards are commonly used with white cedar shingles (see "Corner Boards," page 28), but in traditional

Figure 43. Shingle and Shake Maximum Exposures

Shingle Length	Single Course	Double Course (No. 1)	Double Course (No. 2)
16"	7 1/2"	12"	10"
18"	8 1/2"	14"	11"
24"	11 1/2"	16"	not recommended

Shake Length & Type	Single Course	Double Course (No. 1)
16" machine-grooved	7 1/2"	12"
18" machine-grooved	8 1/2"	14"
18" resawn	8 1/2"	14"
24" resawn	11 1/2"	18"
18" taper-sawn	8 1/2"	14"
24" taper-sawn	11 1/2"	18"
24" tapersplit	11 1/2"	18"
18" straight-split	8 1/2"	16"

The maximum weather exposures for shingles and shakes varies, depending on the length and type of material, as well as on the application (single- or double-course).

requires small, galvanized finish nails to hold the butt joints closed (**Figure 42**, page 45).

Mitering shakes and shingles is not recommended. These corners are likely to open when the siding shrinks, even if nailed.

Inside corners. Flash inside corners with a right-angle flashing extended at least 3 in. under the shingle courses. At a minimum, they should receive an extra layer of building paper.

The simplest inside corner trim is a 1x1 or 2x2 wood strip installed in the corner with the shingles butted against it (**Figure 42**, page 45). Inside corners also may be woven in a manner similar to outside corners — two courses on one side, followed by two courses on the other.

style, shingles or shakes are joined to each other at the corners.

Outside corners. With shakes and red-cedar shingles, corners are often woven with two courses on one side alternating with two courses on the other, each hand-planed to the corner profile. This is labor-intensive and

Weather Exposure

Shingles and shakes may be applied in single or double courses. Double-coursing allows for a greater weather exposure (**Figure 43**).

Double-Coursing

Double-coursing uses two layers of shingles (or one layer of shakes over a layer of No. 3 or No. 4 shingle). This application allows for wider weather exposures, and creates deep shadow lines at the butt ends (**Figure 44**).

Starter Course

Begin with a double underlay course or a single underlay course shimmed out the thickness of a shingle butt with wood lath. Nail undercourse shingles with a single nail in the center.

Face Nail

Double-course applications require face-nailing. Face-nail outer shingles with two nails placed about 2 in. above the butt line and $3/4$ inch in from each end. Shingles wider than 8 in. get two more nails driven near the center, about 1 in. apart. The outer course drops about $1/2$ in. below the undercourse.

Double-Course Variations

Double-course shingles or shakes may also be used over non-wood sheathing (fiberboard or gypsum). In this case,

Figure 44. Double-Coursing

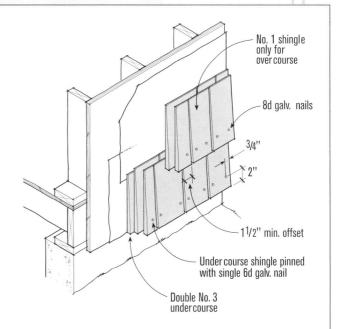

No. 1 shingle only for over course

8d galv. nails

3/4"

2"

1 1/2" min. offset

Under course shingle pinned with single 6d galv. nail

Double No. 3 undercourse

This approach to laying shakes and shingles features wide weather exposures and deep shadow lines. The outer course drops about 1/2 in. below the undercourse, which typically consists of low-grade shingles.

nail strapping below the butt end of the undercourse with 8d box nails, spaced on-center the distance of the weather exposure.

For visual effect, raising the overcourse about 1 in. provides a double shadow line (**Figure 45**). In this case, the undercourse should be a No. 1 grade shingle.

Single-Coursing

Single-coursing is quicker and less expensive because less material is used for a given wall area. However, it requires a narrow weather exposure (**Figure 46**).

Starter Course

Double the first course using inexpensive, lower-grade shingles (No. 3 Black Label or No. 4 Undercoursing).

Blind Nail

Drive nails about 1 in. above the butt line of the course above. For shingles up to 8 in. wide, use two nails per shingle about $3/4$ in. from each edge. For wider shingles, drive two more nails about 1 in. apart near the center (**Figure 47**).

Figure 45. Decorative Coursing Variations

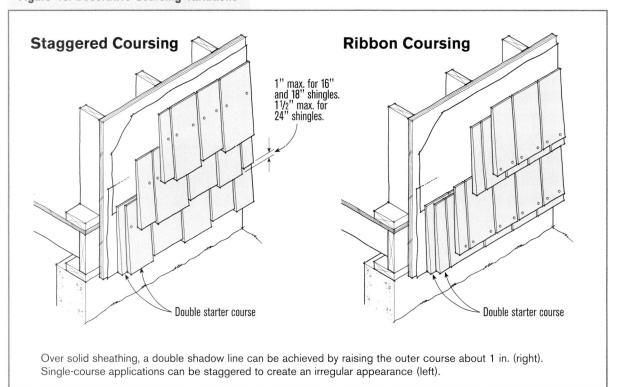

Staggered Coursing

1" max. for 16" and 18" shingles. 1½" max. for 24" shingles.

Double starter course

Ribbon Coursing

Double starter course

Over solid sheathing, a double shadow line can be achieved by raising the outer course about 1 in. (right). Single-course applications can be staggered to create an irregular appearance (left).

Staggered Coursing

For visual effect, butts can be staggered below (not above) the horizontal line (**Figure 45**). The maximum distance to stagger the butts varies with shingle or shake length: Stagger 1 in. for 16s and 18s or $1^1/2$ in. for 24s.

Nailing Checklist

- Install sidewall shingles or shakes with rust-resistant box nails or special shingle nails long enough to penetrate the sheathing (or nailing strips) at least $1/2$- to $3/4$-in. Nails should be hot-dipped galvanized, Type 304 or 316 stainless steel, or high-tensile aluminum.

- Drive nails flush to the shingle or shake surface, but not hard enough to crush the wood fibers, which could split the wood.

- For single-coursing, 3d or 4d shingle nails are commonly used. For double-coursing, 3d or 4d nails are typically used on the undercourse, and 5d box or shingle nails are used on the outer exposed course.

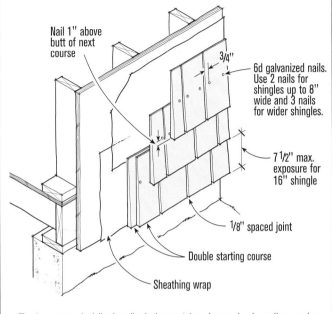

Figure 46. Single-Coursing

Nail 1" above butt of next course

$3/4$"

6d galvanized nails. Use 2 nails for shingles up to 8" wide and 3 nails for wider shingles.

$7^1/2$" max. exposure for 16" shingle

$1/8$" spaced joint

Double starting course

Sheathing wrap

Each course is blind-nailed about 1 in. above the butt line, using two nails for shingles up to 8 in. wide and four nails for larger ones. Offset joints in successive courses by at least $1^1/2$ in.

Shingle and Shake Layout

Shingle Gap

Space all exposed shakes or shingles about $1/8$ in. from each other. This allows room for expansion and gives pieces an individual appearance. Tightly packed shingles that get wet before finishing can buckle.

Offset joints in successive courses by at least $1^1/2$ in. to avoid leakage between shingles.

Aligning Courses

To determine the number of courses, divide the height of the wall into equal parts whose length is not greater than the weather exposure for the shake or shingle. Wherever possible, align shingle butt lines with the tops or bottoms of windows or other openings. This may require adjusting a few courses by a fraction of an inch (**Figure 48**).

Cleaning Shingles and Shakes

Mildew should be removed from shingles before refinishing since it will grow quickly through the new finish.

Figure 47. Preventing Splits in Wide Shingles

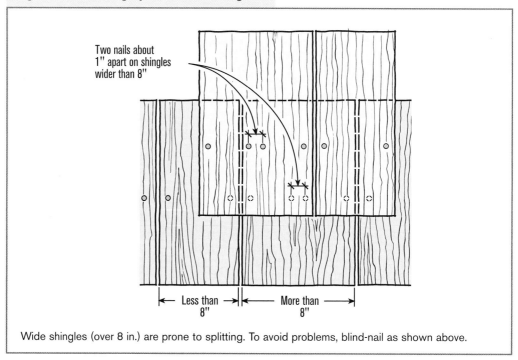

Two nails about 1" apart on shingles wider than 8"

← Less than → 8" ← More than → 8"

Wide shingles (over 8 in.) are prone to splitting. To avoid problems, blind-nail as shown above.

Figure 48. Even Shingle Layout

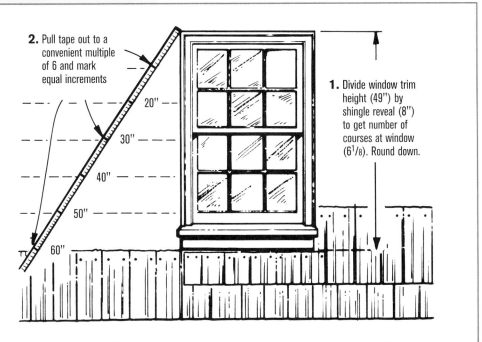

2. Pull tape out to a convenient multiple of 6 and mark equal increments

20"

30"

40"

50"

60"

1. Divide window trim height (49") by shingle reveal (8") to get number of courses at window (6$\frac{1}{8}$). Round down.

To find the number of shingle courses between the top and the bottom of a window: 1) Measure the window height plus the trim. Divide this number by the average shingle exposure. If the resulting number is a fraction, choose the nearest whole number. 2) Hold a tape measure at the corner where the head trim will be, and pull it out to an even multiple. To find the course lines, mark off the even multiples.

To remove mildew, scrub with a solution of 1 cup trisodium phosphate (TSP) dissolved in 1 quart of household bleach mixed with 3 quarts of warm water. Rinse the area thoroughly with clear water, and immediately apply a 50/50 solution of household bleach and water. Allow the last treatment to dry completely before applying any finish. Because bleach can harm skin and eyes, wear protective gloves and goggles during applications and carefully follow manufacturers' instructions.

Vinyl Siding

Figure 49. Locking Edge

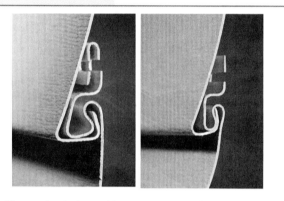

The stiffness of a vinyl panel is more affected by the butt dimension and the lock profile than by the gauge of the vinyl. A square butt (left) will stay straighter and droop less than a post-formed edge.

Figure 50. Nail Hem

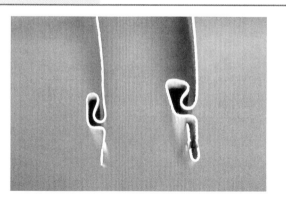

A double-thickness nail hem like the one on the left is less likely to rip in a windstorm.

Vinyl siding is made from extruded PVC (polyvinyl chloride), a durable lightweight plastic. Vinyl siding does not dent, rot, or corrode, and it is manufactured in a wide variety of light colors and textures. Older formulations may be quite brittle from extended exposure to ultraviolet light; however, most formulations nowadays are a co-extrusion of a UV-resistant capstock and a resilient substrate.

Vinyl Siding Types

Typically, vinyl siding is available in horizontally applied panels that simulate lap siding — with one, two, or three siding courses per panel.

V-groove and board-and-batten panels are the most popular forms of vertical vinyl siding. Usually, they are used in combination with horizontal siding on gable ends.

Panel Stiffness

Vinyl thickness varies from about .035 in. (the minimum thickness allowed to comply with the ASTM D3679 standard) to .055 in. While thicker panels are less likely to droop and wave in hot weather, they are not necessarily the best choice, as overlaps between panel lengths are more noticeable with thicker panels. Most installers prefer a "midrange" panel thickness of .042 to .044 in.

The stiffness of panels depends much more on the shape of the panel than on the thickness of the vinyl. The thicker the butt at the locking edge, the stiffer the panel will be and the less likely it will be to droop or wave (**Figure 49**).

Color Choices

While advances in materials science have improved the performance and durability of darker shades of vinyl siding, vinyl is typically available in light colors to reduce surface temperatures. If vinyl gets too hot, it can droop. Also, vinyl chalks as it oxidizes, particularly in humid climates. The white film is more noticeable on darker panels. White siding will be the least likely to show any staining from oxidation.

Wind Resistance

Because vinyl siding must be applied loosely, it may be susceptible to blow-offs. Panels with reinforced nail hems are less likely to be torn off in a storm (**Figure 50**).

Figure 51. Drainage Plane for Vinyl Siding

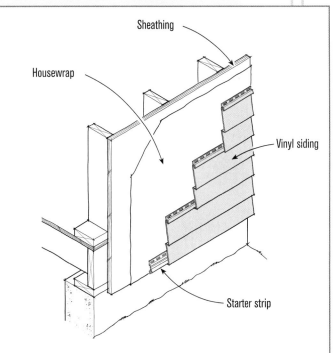

If vinyl siding is nailed loosely (as it should be to accommodate expansion), water that gets behind the siding will be able to drain. A well-detailed sheathing wrap and flashings behind the siding protect the wall from water.

Figure 52. Aluminum Soffit and Fascia Details

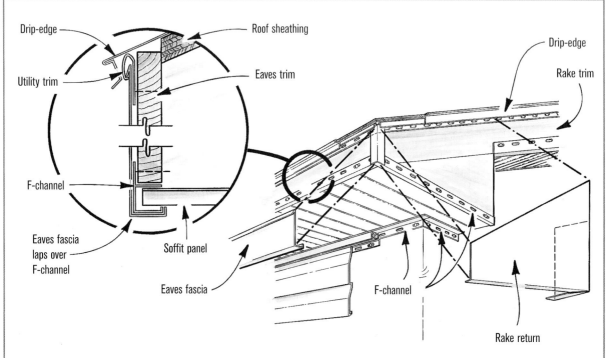

Aluminum trim coil will ripple if nailed. Although small pieces of trim coil may be nailed tight, long lengths of fascia should be secured with utility trim or nails in slotted holes.

Drainage Plane

Of all the siding choices available, vinyl is the only one that does not need extra work to create a drainage gap. Properly nailed, it should hang loose over the wall, allowing water that gets through to drain down and out (**Figure 51, page 53**). However, because vinyl must be installed loosely to accommodate expansion, it's critical to flash and wrap walls carefully (see "Sheathing Wrap and Flashing," page 8).

Trim for Vinyl Siding

Aluminum-covered trim has become the norm in the vinyl siding business. It offers a virtually maintenance-free finish, but how good it looks depends entirely on the skill of the installer.

Figure 52. Aluminum Soffit and Fascia Details, continued

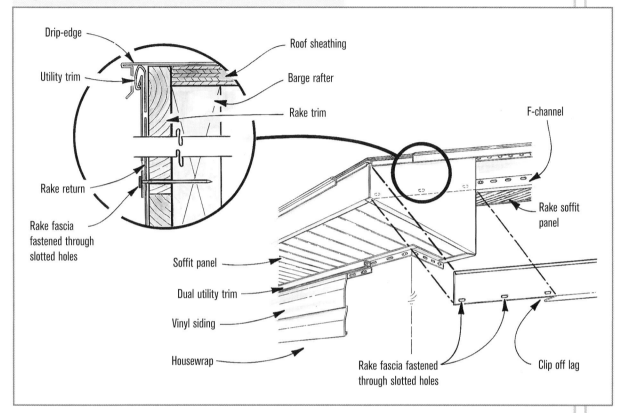

Drip-edge
Roof sheathing
Utility trim
Barge rafter
Rake trim
F-channel
Rake return
Rake soffit panel
Rake fascia fastened through slotted holes
Soffit panel
Dual utility trim
Vinyl siding
Housewrap
Rake fascia fastened through slotted holes
Clip off lag

Trim Coil

Trim is typically bent from two types of aluminum — smooth and striated. Smooth trim coil is a thin aluminum flashing finished with polyester or acrylic paint. Striated coil has a textured finish made with a vinyl paint that forms striated patterns as it dries. Vinyl-coated coil marks up a little easier, requiring a bit more care, but in general the difference is largely a matter of personal preference.

The gauge of almost all aluminum trim coil, whether smooth or striated, is a "nominal" 0.019 in., which can be as thin as .0175 in. and still meet spec. Less common, and about 20% more expensive, is a heavier gauge coil with a nominal measurement of 0.022- to 0.024-in.

Figure 53. Aluminum Fascia Alternatives

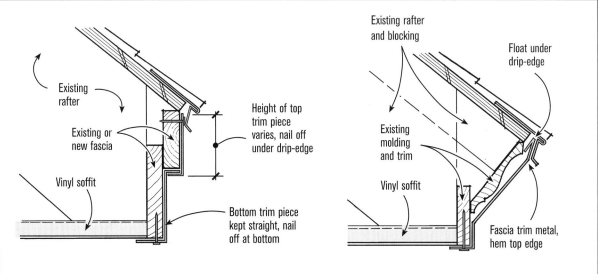

Existing rafter

Existing or new fascia

Vinyl soffit

Height of top trim piece varies, nail off under drip-edge

Bottom trim piece kept straight, nail off at bottom

Existing rafter and blocking

Float under drip-edge

Existing molding and trim

Vinyl soffit

Fascia trim metal, hem top edge

To reduce ripples in aluminum fascia, install a 1x2 to create a two-piece fascia. To keep coil stock stiff, hem the top edge and slip it under the drip-edge.

Trim coil can ripple as it expands in warm weather. This is a problem only if it is face-nailed in cold weather. In addition to limiting face-nailing, try the following to avoid ripples:

- Don't nail too snugly.

- Hem or crease the material to stiffen it.

- Drill or punch an oversized hole in the aluminum before nailing.

- Avoid nailing long fascia and rake pieces. Instead, hold them in place with utility trim and F-channel (**Figure 52**, page 54).

- On rakes and fascias, install a 1x2 at the top of the trim to provide a stepped profile. This stiffens the trim and limits rippling (**Figure 53**).

- To avoid face-nailing a fascia, insert the top of the trim coil under the drip-edge or into a piece of under-sill trim and install a $1^1/4$-in. bend at the bottom toward the soffit. Nail up through the bottom leg every 18- to 24-in.

Figure 54. Trimming a Window

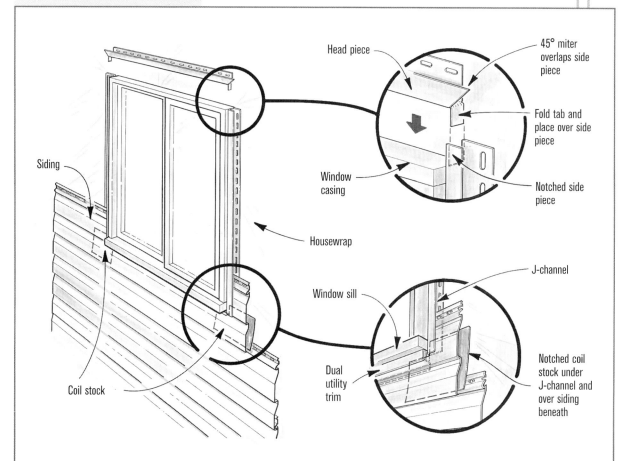

Head piece

45° miter overlaps side piece

Fold tab and place over side piece

Window casing

Notched side piece

Siding

Housewrap

J-channel

Window sill

Dual utility trim

Notched coil stock under J-channel and over siding beneath

Coil stock

When trimming a window, first run J-channel around all four sides. Slip a notched piece of trim coil at each corner of the sill to direct water running down the J-channel over the top of the siding beneath.

Vinyl Window Trim

Window trim is typically framed with J-channel to receive the siding panel (**Figure 54**). The side pieces should be run long enough to receive the mitered head trim (top detail, **Figure 54**), and the sill corners should be flashed with trim coil to divert water running down the J-channel.

Notched wall panels, which have the nail hem ripped off, can be locked in place with dual utility trim (**Figure 55**).

Vinyl Siding Layout

Vinyl siding has a high coefficient of thermal expansion. A 12-ft. length can expand $5/8$ in. from winter to summer. To allow for expansion and contraction of the material, layout is critical.

- Leave a $1/4$ in. gap between corner posts and the soffit.

- Leave a $1/4$-in. gap between the siding and all corner posts and channels

Figure 55. Dual Utility Trim

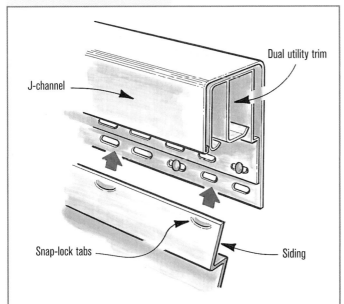

J-channel

Dual utility trim

Snap-lock tabs

Siding

Use dual utility trim to secure notched panels without a nail hem. Use the outer channel for siding panels ripped near to the butt edge; use the inner channel when the rip is made closer to the nail hem.

(**Figure 56**). Increase this gap to $3/8$ in. when installing in temperatures below 40°F.

- Start the layout with a level starter strip. If the foundation is out of level, extend the nailing base as shown in **Figure 57**, page 60.

- Never overlap starter strip, channels, or utility trim. Leave at least $1/4$ in. between pieces to allow for expansion.

- When panels overlap, make sure they overlap by one-half the length of the notch at the end of the panel, or approximately 1 in.

- Stagger the siding end laps so that no two courses (rows of panels) are aligned vertically, unless the laps are separated by at least three courses.

- Plan the direction of siding laps so they face away from high traffic areas. Someone looking into a lap will see a prominent shadow.

Nailing Checklist

- Nail heads should be a minimum $5/16$-in. in diameter, and the shank should be $1/8$ in. in diameter. All fasteners must be able to penetrate at least $3/4$ in. into framing or furring.

- Space nails to hold accessories such as starter strip, J-channel, and utility trim every 8- to 10-in.

- Space siding panel fasteners a maximum of 16 in. apart for the horizontal siding panels, and every 12 in. for vertical panels.

- Lock panels along the bottom edge before nailing top edge. Do not force the panels up or down when fastening.

- While the panel locks should be fully engaged, the panels should not be under vertical tension or compression when they are fastened. An exception can be made at the rim joist between first and second floors. When joists shrink, the panel may be forced down and may unlock, allowing the panel to flap in the wind. Keep some upward tension on the lock at this critical area to account for the shrinkage.

- Start nailing in the center of the panel and work toward the ends.

- Center fasteners in the slots to permit expansion and contraction of the siding. An exception to this rule can be made when fastening vertical siding and corner posts: In this case, start the top nail at the top of the uppermost slot to hold the piece at the proper elevation. All other nails should be centered in the slot.

Figure 56. Corner Treatments for Vinyl Siding

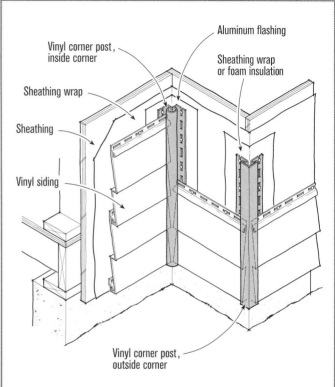

Outside corners (at right) are handled with vinyl corner posts. The corner should be wrapped with foam insulation or sheathing warp first. Inside corners (center) should be flashed with aluminum before installing the siding.

- Do not drive the head of the fastener tightly against the siding nail hem. Leave a minimum of $1/32$ in. (the thickness of a dime) between the fastener head and the vinyl (**Figure 58**).

Figure 57. Starting Out Level

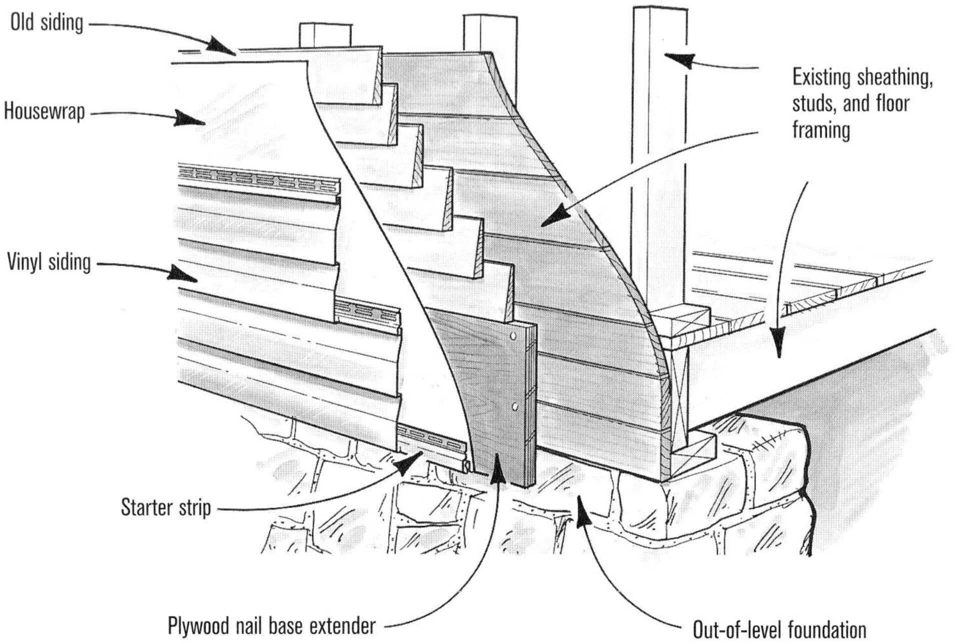

Old siding

Housewrap

Vinyl siding

Existing sheathing, studs, and floor framing

Starter strip

Plywood nail base extender

Out-of-level foundation

Siding should be installed level. When foundations are out of level, extend the nail base with a piece of plywood that matches the thickness of existing siding.

Cutting Vinyl Siding

Cut vinyl panels with a fine-toothed (plywood) blade mounted backwards on the saw for a smoother, cleaner cut. This works especially well in cold weather when cutting with snips may crack the panel.

When cutting with tin snips, avoid closing the blades completely at the end of a stroke for a neater, cleaner cut.

Cleaning Vinyl Siding

To clean vinyl siding, use a long-handled brush with soft bristles (such as a car washing brush), and a handle that fastens onto the end of the hose. Avoid using stiff bristle brushes or abrasive cleaners, which may change the vinyl's gloss and cause the siding to look splotchy.

When cleaning soot and dust from the house, use the following cleaning

Figure 58. Nailing Vinyl Siding

Do not drive nails home when installing vinyl siding. Vinyl siding needs to be able to slide back and forth as it expands and contracts with changes in temperature.

Figure 59. Stain Cleaners for Vinyl Siding

Stain	Cleaner*
Bubble Gum	Fantastik®, Murphy's Oil Soap®, or solution of vinegar (30%) + water (70%)
Crayon	Lestoil®
Oil-based caulk	Fantastik®
Felt-tip pen	Fantastik® or water-based cleaners
Grass	Fantastik®, Lysol®, Murphy's Oil Soap®, or Windex®
Lipstick	Fantastik® or Murphy's Oil Soap®
Lithium grease	Fantastik®, Lestoil®, Murphy's Oil Soap®, or Windex®
Mold and mildew	Fantastik® or solution of vinegar (30%) + water (70%)
Motor oil	Fantastik®, Lysol®, Murphy's Oil Soap®, or Windex®
Oil	Soft Scrub®
Paint	Brillo® Pad or Soft Scrub®
Pencil	Soft Scrub®
Rust	Fantastik®, Murphy's Oil Soap®, or Windex®
Tar	Soft Scrub®
Soil	Fantastik®, Lestoil®, or Murphy's Oil Soap®

*Cleaning materials are listed in alphabetical order.

Courtesy of Vinyl Siding Institute

solution, starting at the bottom and working up to the top in order to prevent streaking:

- 1/3 cup powdered laundry detergent, such as Fab®, Tide®, or equivalent*

- 2/3 cup powdered household cleaner, such as Soilax®, Spic &Span®, or equivalent*

- 1 gallon water

To remove mildew, add 1 qt. liquid laundry bleach to the solution above. Clean stubborn stains using the recommended cleaners shown in **Figure 59**.

Fiber-Cement Siding

The main ingredients in fiber-cement are Portland cement, sand, and wood fiber; essentially, it's a masonry product, and nearly as durable. It won't burn, rot, or be eaten by insects, and it is dimensionally stable. Unlike wood and wood-composites, such as hardboard, it won't cup, shrink, or swell, and it holds paint exceptionally well. Fiber-cement siding typically carries a 50-year warranty.

Figure 60. Starter Strip for Lap Siding

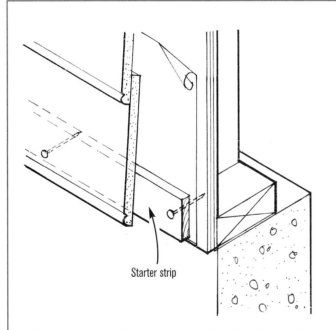

Starter strip

The first course of fiber-cement lap siding should be applied over a 1/4-in.-thick starter strip. Extend the siding 1/2 in. below the starter strip.

Fiber-Cement Types

Fiber-cement siding is available as lap siding (12-ft. lengths from $5^1/4$- to 12-in. wide), shingle panels (16x48-in.), and vertical or stucco-like panels (4x8, 4x9, and 4x10).

Handling Fiber-Cement

Fiber-cement siding is a lot heavier than wood of comparable thickness. The $5/16$-in.-thick material weighs about $2^1/4$ pounds per sq. ft., making it difficult to handle when working alone. It's also quite flexible, and full-length pieces can snap under their own weight. Always carry boards on edge rather than on the flat.

Aluminum/Cement Conflict

Any cementitious material, including fiber-cement siding, can attack aluminum if the aluminum is not protected. Aluminum trim should be anodized. Most window manufacturers anodize their aluminum trim. To be safe, prime the ends of the siding at field cuts near aluminum windows or flashing.

Trim for Fiber-Cement

Fiber-cement trim and soffit panels are available. Because the material is so heavy, trim stock is typically only $7/16$-in.-thick. It does not provide a good nail base for built-up trim and cannot provide deep shadow lines, so it requires the use of wood trim. For information about detailing exterior wood trim, see "Wood Trim," page 24.

Layout for Fiber-Cement Siding

- Apply a level starter strip under the first course of lap siding (**Figure 60**).
- Overlap courses at least $1^1/4$ in.

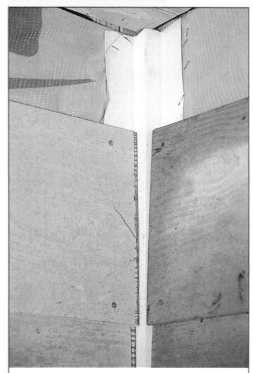

Figure 61. Inside Corners for Fiber-Cement Siding

Where joints fall between studs, apply metal joiner plates onto the butt ends of the siding. These should not be fastened to the wall.

- Butt lap siding against vertical trim pieces at inside corners. Wood 2x2s can be used, but vinyl corner trim, available from Tamlyn and Sons (800/334-1676, www.tamlyn.com), is preferred (**Figure 61**).
- Join lap siding over a stud. If the butt joint falls between studs, use an off-stud joiner plate (**Figure 62**).

Figure 62. Off-Stud Joiner Plates

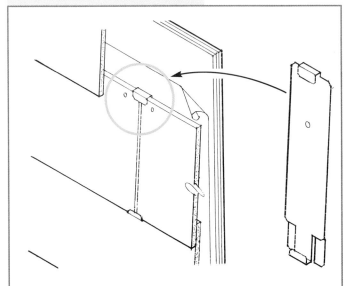

Vinyl inside corner trims, which are similar in profile to a W valley flashing, are designed specifically for use with fiber-cement lap siding. Once painted, they look just like wood.

holding power and voids the warranty.

- Narrower lap siding (up to $9^1/2$ in. wide) can be blind-nailed with a wide-head, .121-in.-shank roofing nail. While this looks better, it is not recommended in high wind areas.

- Wider panels must be face-nailed at the bottom edge with 6d nails (minimum .093-in. shank with a .267-in. head diameter). This effectively pins each panel down with nails along both edges since the face nail penetrates the underlapping piece as well (**Figure 63**).

- Fasteners must penetrate 1- to $1^1/4$-in. into framing (including sheathing).

- Use only corrosion-resistant round-head nails (not clipped-head nails or staples).

- Leave a $1/8$-in. gap between the siding and the edge of wood casings and corner boards. This gap is necessary to allow for settlement and dimensional changes in wood framing. The joint should be sealed with caulk.

Nailing Checklist

- The most important caution when nailing fiber-cement is to avoid overdriving fasteners. The siding is only $5/16$ in. thick, so setting nail heads below the surface decreases

Cutting Fiber-Cement

Fiber-cement can be cut with carbide or abrasive circular saw blades. Fiber-cement is hard on saws and produces serious clouds of dust. Toothed carbide blades cut faster and produce less dust than abrasive blades, but the carbide tips dull fairly quickly.

Figure 63. Nailing Fiber-Cement Siding

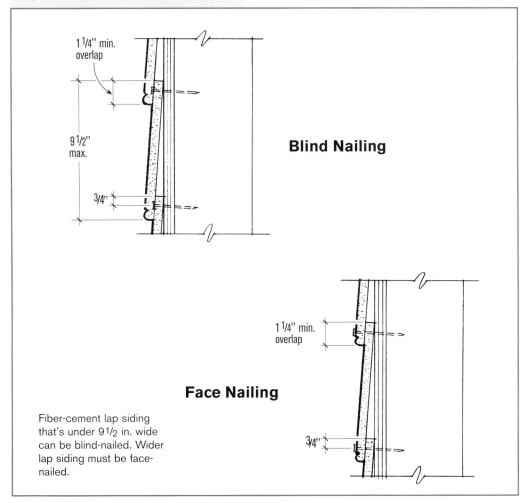

1 1/4" min. overlap

9 1/2" max.

3/4"

Blind Nailing

1 1/4" min. overlap

Face Nailing

Fiber-cement lap siding that's under 9 1/2 in. wide can be blind-nailed. Wider lap siding must be face-nailed.

3/4"

An alternative is to use Pacific International's Snapper Lite shears (Pacific International Tool and Shear, Ltd., 800/297-7487, www.snappers-hear.com). These work like motorized tin snips, and while they are slower than a circular saw, they can make straight and curved cuts without producing much dust.

Hardboard Siding

Hardboard is a homogenized wood product made from a wood fiber pulp formed into panels or lap pieces under high heat and pressure.

Figure 64. H-Trim for Hardboard Siding

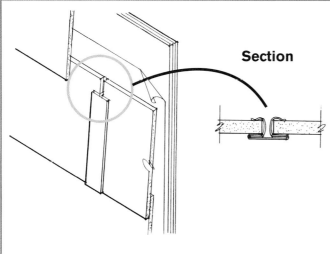

Section

Butt joints between siding panels should be joined with color-matched, metal H-trim. This aluminum trim covers the vulnerable ends of the material without relying on caulk.

Hardboard Grades

Hardboard siding comes in $3/8$-, $7/16$-, and $1/2$-in. thicknesses. In general, the $1/2$-in. product performs better than the thinner versions.

At least five different grades are available. The better quality sidings are of "tempered" grade, which is impregnated with additives and/or is heat-treated to make it stiffer, harder, and more resistant to water and abrasion.

Nearly all hardboard siding today comes primed and ready to paint or stain. About 10% of hardboard siding is sold pre-finished for quicker installation.

Hardboard Siding Patterns

Hardboard is available to mimic nearly every siding style, but it falls into two basic categories: lap siding and panel siding.

Lap profiles, designed to look like cedar, redwood, or fir clapboards, account for 60% of hardboard sales. Boards come in standard 16-ft. lengths, ranging in width from 4- to 16-in.-wide, as well as wider "multilap" versions that will take care of several "rows" of siding at once.

Hardboard siding also comes in 2x8, 2x10, 4x8, and 4x9 panels, which install quickly. The panels imitate everything from board-and-batten construction to stone and stucco.

Drainage Plane

Because hardboard is so vulnerable to moisture, it's imperative to install it over a drainage plane — either a rain-screen mat or battens. Follow the guidelines outlined for "Board Siding, Drainage Plane," page 39.

Installing Hardboard Siding

Hardboard comes from the factory at a low moisture content (below 10%), so it must acclimate to job-site conditions. Otherwise, it will pick up moisture and expand (**Figure 35**, page 34).

Figure 65. Corner Treatments for Hardboard Siding

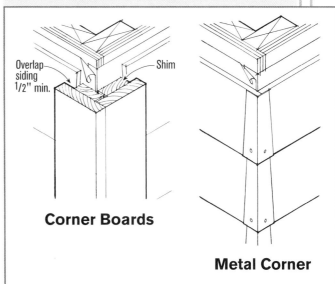

Overlap siding 1/2" min.

Shim

Corner Boards

Metal Corner

To protect the cut ends of hardboard panels, use rabbeted corner boards or color-matched metal corners. Do not leave cut ends exposed or they will absorb moisture and swell.

Also, because hardboard is a homogenized wood, it expands more in length than a piece of solid wood siding does, and it will buckle if it's nailed down and then expands.

Avoid installing hardboard siding when a building's concrete foundation is still green, or when the building is excessively wet from fresh plaster, wet-spray insulation, or other wet materials.

Hardboard Siding Checklist

Because hardboard is vulnerable to moisture damage, quality of installation is critical to its performance. To stray from the manufacturer's installation guidelines is asking for trouble and can void the warranty. Installation guidelines vary only slightly from one manufacturer to another.

To avoid problems caused by moisture:

- Leave gaps of about $1/8$ in. between butt ends of boards and between boards and trim. This gap will provide maximum hold for an exterior caulk (see "Caulks and Sealants," page 100). Caulk should be primed and painted with two topcoats. Keep caulk joints to a minimum; they will be the first point of failure in the paint job.

- To limit caulk joints, cover butt joints between panel lengths with a special "H-trim" (see **Figure 64**, page 66).

- Use galvanized box nails driven flush with the board's surface. Do not break the siding, or the hole will absorb moisture and will pucker.

- Cut with a fine-tooth saw blade. Always cut into the face of the board: Place boards face up when using a hand saw, or face down when using a circular saw.

- Outside corner boards and trim should be rabbetted. If a mitered corner is desired, cover the joint with color-matched metal corners (**Figure 65**, page 67). At the very least, use $5/4$ trim that is thick enough to completely cover the ends and edges of the siding.

- Do not install hardboard siding closer than 6 or 8 in. to the ground, or closer than 2 in. to roofs. In areas where it snows a lot, leave a 4- or 6- in. gap above roofs intersecting the walls.

- Paint all field cuts to help seal the ends. This is particularly important above intersecting roofs.

- Apply finish to the siding within 30- to -90 days after installation (see "Finishes," page 103).

Stucco

Stucco is mostly sand and Portland cement. Traditionally, it is applied in three separate coats that add up, more or less, to $7/8$ in. for one-hour fire-rated construction.

Stucco Types

Traditional Three-Coat Stucco

Three-coat stucco consists of three separate layers of cement plaster materials: a trowel-applied scratch coat, which is applied over lath and grooved to provide a key way for the next coat; a sand-finished brown coat, which keys into the scratch coat; and a cementitious finish, or color coat (**Figure 66**).

One-Coat Stucco

Often known as thin-coat stucco or fiberglass reinforced stucco (FRS), one-coat systems have some distinct advantages. "One-coat" is somewhat of a misnomer as it actually requires two coats: a single, thin base coat, followed by a cementitious color coat or one of the newer acrylic-based synthetic color coats.

Figure 66. Drainage Plane for Three-Coat Stucco

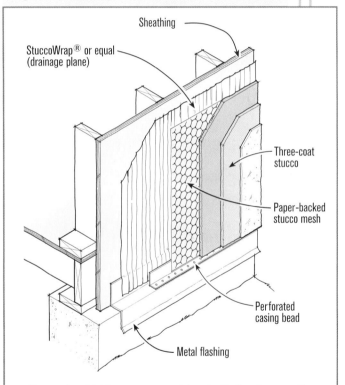

Stucco is a highly porous material and will absorb water. To protect the structure against water damage, apply a "wrinkle wrap" type drainage plane and proper flashings so water can drain down and out.

Figure 67. Drainage Plane for Synthetic Stucco

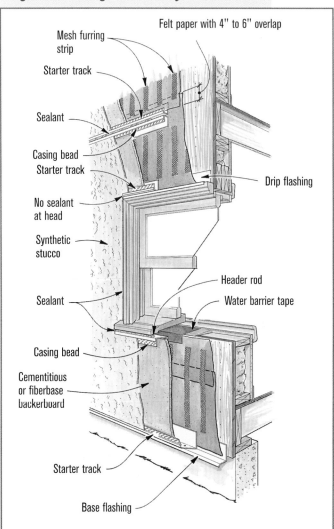

Cementitious backerboard provides a more durable substrate for synthetic stucco than foam insulation board. The backerboard must be installed over mesh furring strips to provide a drainage gap so that any water that gets through the stucco is directed to weep areas at windows and wall skirts.

EIFS

Exterior insulation and finish system (EIFS), is an acrylic stucco finish applied over a rigid insulation board, such as extruded polystyrene sheathing. The original intent of this material was to create a watertight skin using sealants and control joints. In practice, this system proved impractical without impeccable detailing, and many problems — leading to many lawsuits — ensued. Most successful synthetic stucco systems used today are applied over a drainage plane using cementitious backerboard, rather than foam insulation, as the substrate (**Figure 67**).

Drainage Plane

Stucco of any type will crack, even under the best of conditions. Even synthetic stucco, which is more elastic than other stucco types, is still intolerant to movement in the underlying surface. Movement is a bigger problem on wood-framed walls than on block, insulated block, and poured concrete. However, no structure is immune to settlement or movement caused by changing climate conditions. All stucco systems should be applied over a drainage plain (**Figure 66** and **Figure 67**).

Sheathing Wrap for Stucco

All stucco systems require sheathing wrap — either two layers of Type D paper (the minimum allowed by code) or No. 15 felt paper, or a single layer of "wrinkle wrap," such as StuccoWrap®. StuccoWrap bends more easily than black paper and is less likely to tear during installation. Paper-backed lath should not be considered a substitute for well-detailed sheathing wrap.

Lap lower courses of sheathing wrap under upper courses so water will drain down and out, and flash all openings, following the flashing guidelines found in "Flashing Details," page 17.

Weep Screeds and Control Joints

A perforated weep screed at the bottom of the wall and over openings serves two important purposes — it provides a screed that helps ensure a uniform coat thickness, and it provides a place for water that leaks into the wall to escape (**Figure 68**).

Stucco Control Joints

Control joints allow for structural movements that would otherwise crack the stucco. On a house, control

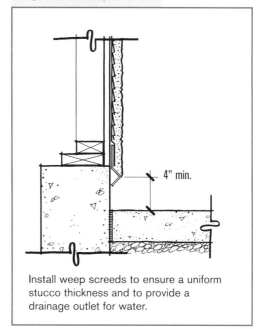

Figure 68. Weep Screed

4" min.

Install weep screeds to ensure a uniform stucco thickness and to provide a drainage outlet for water.

joints should be applied over the metal lath at a few critical locations:

- Over the rim joist at the intersection between floors to accommodate shrinkage in the floor joists

- Over the intersection between different types of construction, such as the joint between wood framing and a block wall (**Figure 69**)

- On tall walls and long runs, applied vertically or horizontally to break up wall areas into smaller sections (less than 18 ft.)

Similarly, casing bead and corner bead help to create expansion joints at critical intersections:

Figure 69. Stucco Control Joints

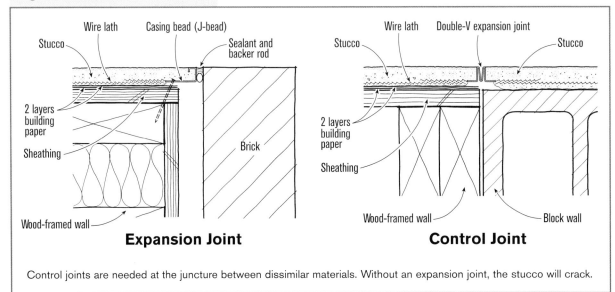

Control joints are needed at the juncture between dissimilar materials. Without an expansion joint, the stucco will crack.

- Outside corners are best detailed with corner bead (**Figure 70**). Continuous stucco wrapped around corners is likely to crack.

- Inside corners should be flashed with two layers of sheathing wrap or flexible flashing, and then casing bead should be applied vertically to create an expansion joint (**Figure 70**). While the flashing serves as the most important water-sealing protection, the joint between the two casing beads should be caulked with a high-quality urethane caulk as a first-line defense.

- Apply casing bead (also called J bead) at the joint between any dissimilar materials — around window flanges (**Figure 67,** page 70), where stucco meets a brick chimney (**Figure 69**), or at the top of a wall where stucco meets a soffit or frieze board.

Metal Lath

Traditional three-coat systems and one-coat systems both require lath — either expanded metal lath or wire lath

(**Figure 71**). The primary purpose of metal lath is to provide a keyway to bond the stucco to the structure, and so it must stand off the wall slightly to allow stucco to get behind it and fully encase the metal. This is done by using a self-furring material or with furring nails. Metal lath also provides some tension reinforcement for the stucco, but it will not prevent cracking. Cracking must be controlled by using the right mix, controlling the temperature during application, and allowing the stucco to cure.

Expanded metal lath comes in several varieties. Diamond lath is available in plain, self-furring (allows plaster underneath the lath), and paper-backed. Stucco mesh is similar to diamond lath but has larger openings. It is available only plain, so it must be installed with furring nails over sheathing wrap. Flat-ribbed lath typically requires furring nails; it is available in two weights — 2.75- and 3.4-lbs.-per-yd. The lighter material is made for interior plaster and is not suitable for exterior stucco. Three-eighths-inch rib lath is self-furring, but it is difficult to encase completely in stucco and is not recommended for wet climates.

Wire lath is not the same as chicken wire. Woven wire is available in plain,

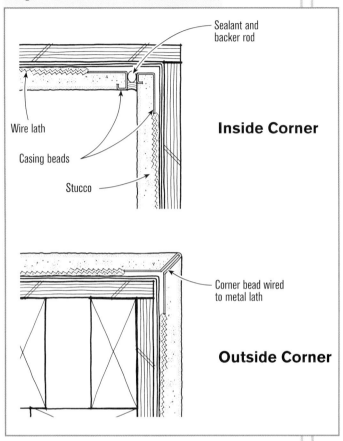

Figure 70. Stucco Corner Treatments

Sealant and backer rod

Wire lath

Casing beads

Stucco

Inside Corner

Corner bead wired to metal lath

Outside Corner

self-furring, and paper-backed versions; plain wire lath should be installed with furring nails. Use heavier 16- and 17-gauge material for three-coat stucco; lighter 20-gauge wire can be used for one-coat systems.

Furring nails. When using plain lath, use furring fasteners — which have fiber spacers — to keep the lath about 1/4 in. away from the sheathing wrap.

Figure 71. Metal Lath for Stucco

	Type	Weight (lb. per sq. yd.)	Opening Size (in.)	Typical Unit Dimensions
Expanded Metal	Diamond mesh*	1.75, 2.5 and 3.4	$5/16$ x $3/8$	27 in. x 96 in.
	$1/8$-in. flat rib mesh*	2.75 and 3.4	$5/16$ x $3/8$	27 in. x 96 in.
	$3/8$-in. rib lath (high rib)	3.4 and 4.0	$5/16$ x $3/8$	27 in. x 96 in.
Wire Lath	Woven wire**	1.7 (18 gauge)	1 (hexagonal)	3 ft. x 150 ft. (rolls)**
		1.4 (17 gauge)	$1^1/2$ (hexagonal)	3 ft. x 150 ft. (rolls)**
	Welded wire**	1.4 (16 gauge)	2 x 2	3 ft. x 150 ft. (rolls)**
		1.4 (18 gauge)	1 x 1	3 ft. x 150 ft. (rolls)**
		1.9 (16 gauge)	$1^1/2$ x 2	3 ft. x 150 ft. (rolls)**

*Available in plain, self-furring, and paper-backed
**Paper-backed and self-furring also available in sheets

This allows the stucco to fully encase the lath.

Installing Metal Lath

- Run the long dimension of metal lath perpendicular to the framing.

- With plain (unbacked) lath, start at the top so lower courses lap over upper courses. Paper-backed sheets should be the opposite — "shingled" so upper courses lap over lower courses, like the sheathing wrap, allowing water to drain down and out.

- Expanded metal lath should be lapped $1/2$ in. along the top and bottom sides and 1 in. at the ends. Wire lath should be lapped on all sides at least one full mesh (1- to 2-in.).

- Use galvanized fasteners. Do not use aluminum fasteners; these will react galvanically with the steel lath.

Three-Coat Stucco

The first two coats of a three-coat system are made of a site-mixed cement plaster. Each batch contains measured amounts of Portland cement, hydrated lime, fine sand, and water. To help reduce the cracking that is common with stucco, the basic mix can be modified with liquid polymer additives, which increase strength and improve curing, and with chopped fiberglass for reinforcement.

Scratch Coat

The scratch coat is applied directly to a clean block wall or, on wood structures, over "D" paper (or better) and galvanized metal lath. A metal rake is used to create "scratch" lines in the still-wet surface. The furrows create a rough surface into which the brown coat can key for a good bond.

Scratch-coat thickness. The scratch coat should be approximately 3/8- to 1/2-in. thick — thick enough to just cover the wire.

Brown Coat

The brown coat (which is actually gray, like other cement stucco) is applied the next day as a smooth coat, usually "rodded" with straightedges and wooden floats (**Figure 72**). In the western U.S., a steel trowel is used to produce an adobe look when the brown coat is the final coat.

Brown-coat thickness. The brown coat is composed of slightly more sand than the scratch coat mixture, and therefore it is more manageable but

Figure 72. Brown Coat

A $1/4$- to $3/8$-in.-thick brown coat is applied over the scratch coat and "rodded" with a straightedge.

slightly weaker. It should be applied $1/4$- to $3/8$-in. thick. Apply the brown coat as evenly as possible. An uneven brown coat can lead to an inconsistent thickness in the finish coat, causing some areas of the finish coat to dry before others. The result is a splotchy or "mottled" color coat and excessive hairline cracking.

Once applied, the two coats should be allowed to cure for at least a week, preferably two weeks, before applying the finish coat (see "Curing Stucco,"

Figure 73. Finish Coat

A $^1/8$-in.-thick finish coat is applied with a trowel.

page 80). This allows the scratch and brown coats to strengthen, settle down, and do all the shrinkage cracking they intend to do.

Finish Coat

After the curing period, a finish coat can be applied (**Figure 73**). Color is applied to the finish mix by adding iron oxide pigments to a mix made with white Portland cement. There are many types of pigments available at different prices. The cheaper pigments tend to fade and be inconsistent from batch to batch.

Finish-coat thickness. The finish coat is only about $^1/8$ in. thick. It should be applied as evenly as possible to ensure uniform drying.

Mixing Stucco

Stucco (like concrete) derives its strength as a result of two factors: the relative strength of the mix and its drying time. A wet mixture will result in excessive shrinkage (often called checking), and a dry mixture — or stucco completed in very hot weather — will create a weak bond (see "Weather Precautions," page 79).

Stucco Ingredients

Water

Use clean water that is suitable for drinking. Mineral and organic impurities in water may discolor or affect the set time, and may attack metal lath.

Sand

It is important to use bagged silica sand to ensure that there are no iron particles in the mix, which may cause staining. Do not use the less expensive "yard sand," which often has impurities.

Figure 74. Stucco Mixes

Group	Mix Proportions (parts per volume)				
	Portland Cement	**Type II Masonry Cement**	**Plastic Cement**	**Lime**	**Sand**
C (Cement)	1	–	–	0 to $1/4$	3 to 4
C	1	1	–	–	6 to $7^1/2$
C	1	–	–	$1/4$ to $1/2$	4 to 6
L (Lime)	1	–	–	2 to $1^1/4$	$4^1/2$ to 9
L	–	1	–	–	3 to 4
F (Finish)	1	–	–	$1^1/4$ to 2	5 to 10
P (Plastic)	1	–	1	–	6 to 10
P	–	–	1	–	3 to 4

Base Material	Recommended Stucco Group		
	Scratch	**Brown***	**Finish**
Low Absorption (poured concrete, dense brick)	C, P	C, L, P	L, F, P
High Absorption (concrete block, clay brick structural tile)	L, P	L, P	L, F, P
Metal Reinforcement (over all types of construction)	C, P	C, L, P	L, F, P

* Use as base coat in two-coat work.

Choose the stucco group for each coat, depending on the base material requirement shown in the bottom half of this table. When mixing each stucco group, keep proportions consistent between batches and follow mix proportions shown in the top half of the table.

Adapted from Portland Cement Association

Cement

Most stucco uses Portland cement or masonry cement. White Portland cement is used to produce a white or light-colored finish coat. Plastic cement is a special cement made expressly for the plaster industry, and is commonly available in the Southwest and on the West coast. It is a blend of Portland cement and plasticizing materials, such as limestone or hydrated lime. When plastic cement is used, no lime or other plasticizer is required.

Figure 75. Curing Schedule for Cement Stucco

Stucco Coat	Moist Curing	Total Setting Time*
Scratch	12 to 24 hr.	At least 48 hr. (between coats)
Brown	12 to 24 hr.	At least 7 days (between coats)
Finish**	12 to 24 hr.	At least 48 hr. (before painting)

* Air temperature min. 50°F should be maintained during this time.

** Moisten base coat immediately before applying finish coat.

Plasticizer

The function of a plasticizer is to improve the workability of the brown and finish coats or the scratch coats applied over poured concrete walls. Type S hydrated lime is the most common plasticizer used in stucco.

Mix Proportions

Inconsistent mixing will result in obvious differences in color, texture, and strength between batches. Over time, mismixed batches can effloresce or fail. Make every effort to keep mix proportions consistent, following the guidelines shown in **Figure 74**, page 77.

Mixing Procedure

Follow this procedure, using a paddle-type mortar mixer:

- Add majority of the mix water and start mixer. Keep in mind that the drier the mix, the stronger the stucco, so don't add too much water.

- Add approximately half of the sand.

- Add lime (if required), followed by cement and any admixtures required.

- Add remainder of sand.

- Add pigment (finish coats only). Allow the mixer to run until the color is dispersed throughout the entire load. Undermixing the finish will permit lumps of raw color to be left in the finish.

- Add water required to reach desired consistency (and no more). Continue mixing 3 to 5 minutes until batch is mixed uniformly.

- Keep batches to a size that can be applied within one hour after mixing.

Weather Precautions

Cold Weather

Don't mix materials or apply stucco when the air temperature is below 35°F. Keep materials covered at night, and if working temperatures are low, warm the mix water and the sand with salamander heaters. Also keep freezing rain and snow away from freshly stuccoed walls. If possible, install gutters and tip up scaffold planks at the end of the day to reduce splashback.

A calcium-based accelerant can be added as an "anti-freeze." But this also increases the salinity of the mix and may cause efflorescence — the migration of salts to the surface.

Hot Weather

In hot or warm, windy weather (above 75°F), there is a danger of the stucco drying too fast, or flash curing. Keep materials out of the direct sun. Sand and water both hold heat, and if these can be kept cool, the stucco will dry more slowly. But don't moisten the sand to cool it off; this may throw off the mix ratio. If possible, start work early in the day and "chase the shadows" (working in the shade will slow drying times).

Figure 76. Common Stucco Textures

Sand Float
After troweling on stucco, use a sponge float in a swirling motion. Additional water may be sprinkled lightly on the area, as needed, to roll the sand, but don't over-rub; this may create a bald spot.

Fine Lace
Use a small brush and lightly dab wet stucco onto the colored stucco base. Wait a minute for the excess water to dry out, and then flatten the ridges by lightly running a clean trowel over the dabbed spots.

Smooth Finish
Trowel on the finish stucco, continually working and smoothing the material. To reduce small shrinkage cracks, it may be necessary to retrowel a second and third time, sprinkling water on the wall with a brush, as needed, to act as a lubricant for the trowel.

After applying brown coat, keep freshly stuccoed walls damp in hot weather, using a garden sprayer or a garden hose with a fogging head. Mist the walls every hour until the sun and wind are no longer a problem. Also, draping new work with wet burlap and keeping a soaker hose on the top of the wall to keep the burlap wet will retard evaporation as well.

Do not mist or dampen a color coat, however. This may result in splotchy walls. To be safe, the only choice is to wait for the right weather to apply the finish coat.

Figure 77. Drainage EIFS Details

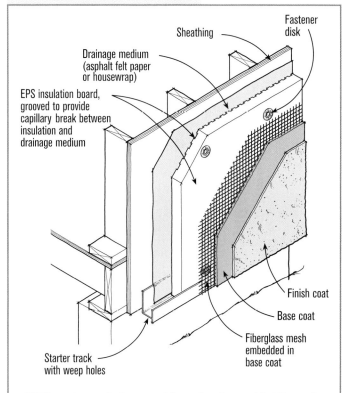

- Sheathing
- Fastener disk
- Drainage medium (asphalt felt paper or housewrap)
- EPS insulation board, grooved to provide capillary break between insulation and drainage medium
- Finish coat
- Base coat
- Fiberglass mesh embedded in base coat
- Starter track with weep holes

EIFS can be applied on wood-framed walls, provided the wall is designed to drain when the stucco cracks. The drainage plane relies on well-detailed sheathing wrap and flashing, and a grooved EPS insulation board.

Curing Stucco

The brown and scratch coats must cure for a minimum of seven days before the color coat can be applied (**Figure 75**, page 78). For best results, wait four weeks to allow the brown coat to achieve full strength.

Three-coat stucco requires moist curing — fogging with fine water spray at the beginning and the end of the work day under normal weather conditions. Fogging should be delayed until the scratch and brown coats are sufficiently set to prevent erosion, and at least 12 hours after applying the finish coat. For two-coat stucco applications, follow curing recommendations for brown and finish coats.

Finish Textures

The color-coat finish is usually floated to a sand finish, but an experienced applicator can vary the texture and color with trowel techniques (**Figure 76,** page 79).

One-Coat Stucco

Base coat. One-coat stucco uses a single factory-prepared base coat, consisting of fiberglass-reinforced cement plaster with modifying polymers. Sand and water are the only additions on the job site.

Color coat. Synthetic stucco finishes come pre-mixed in five-gallon buckets. These products primarily use an acrylic polymer base (much like exterior latex paint, but more flexible and durable) mixed with fine aggregate and pigment. Synthetic finishes can be tinted to almost any color and are not subject to shade variations.

Pros

One-coat systems offer several advantages. Factory batching of the base and color coats helps eliminate much of the variation that can occur with batching three-coat mixes. It also speeds up application by eliminating the need to work to corners in warm weather because drying time does not affect the final color. In addition to eliminating one coat altogether, less curing time is required for the base coat. In a pinch, a cementitious finish coat can go on after 48 hours, or a synthetic

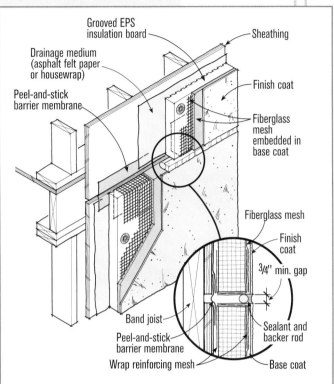

Figure 78. EIFS Control Joints

Grooved EPS insulation board — Sheathing

Drainage medium (asphalt felt paper or housewrap)

Peel-and-stick barrier membrane

Finish coat

Fiberglass mesh embedded in base coat

Fiberglass mesh

Finish coat

3/4" min. gap

Band joist

Peel-and-stick barrier membrane

Wrap reinforcing mesh

Sealant and backer rod

Base coat

EPS board in an EIFS system can buckle when floor framing shrinks. Build a way for the board to move by creating a 3/4-in. gap between upper and lower sheathing panels and upper and lower EPS boards. Seal the gap over the sheathing with peel-and-stick flashing, and seal the gap in the insulation with backer rod and silicone sealant.

color coat can go on after just 24 hours. However, it is usually better to wait at least seven days, if possible, to allow the base coat to reach its full strength and complete all shrinkage cracking.

Figure 79. Kickout Flashing for Synthetic Stucco

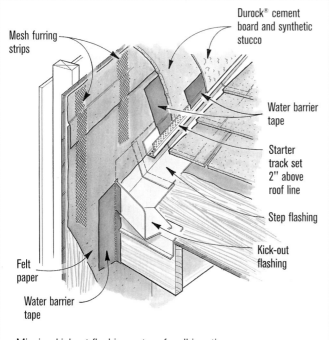

Mesh furring strips

Durock® cement board and synthetic stucco

Water barrier tape

Starter track set 2" above roof line

Step flashing

Kick-out flashing

Felt paper

Water barrier tape

Missing kickout flashings at roof-wall junctions are a common source of EIFS failures. Use a flashing metal of the same type as the drip-edge to avoid galvanic corrosion.

Cons

On the downside, one-coat stucco is not as impact-resistant as three-coat stucco. Also, the finish appearance of a one-coat stucco job is so uniform and monochromatic that it may not perfectly capture the three-coat stucco look some clients have in mind. Nor will a one-coat finish last as long. Most manufacturers claim a 15-year finish, whereas a traditional color coat on a three-coat stucco, properly applied, will last 20 to 30 years.

EIFS

EIFS (Exterior Insulated Finish System) was originally developed for use on concrete buildings in Europe. The original system — known as barrier EIFS — depends on an extruded polystyrene (EPS) insulation board that is glued to the wall, helping to prevent movement of the substrate. This detail was lost when it was applied to wood-framed buildings in the U.S. Stucco of any kind is bound to crack and allow water to intrude — a problem that has more serious consequences on a wood-framed structure than on a concrete one. On wood-framed structures, a drainage EIFS (also called water-managed EIFS) is required.

Drainage EIFS Design

• Provide a complete secondary weather barrier with a water-shedding drainage plane and flashings (**Figure** 77, page 80).

• Provide sealed movement joints at floors (**Figure** 78, page 81).

• All penetrations should be flashed beneath the EIFS with peel-and-stick flexible flashing (see "Flexible Flashing Materials," page 13), as well as a surface-seal at the joint with backer rod and silicone sealant (see "Caulks and Sealants," page 100).

- At wall-roof junctions, provide kickout flashings at roof terminations on sidewalls (**Figure 79**).

- Provide Z-shaped counterflashing along sidewalls (**Figure 80**) and two-piece head flashings on front walls (**Figure 81**).

- Provide sill flashings at windows (**Figure 11**, page 10).

Drainage EIFS Materials

- Use only high-density, low-porosity EPS board with grooves to provide drainage.

- Use wet-mix base coats, not dry mixes.

- Use 6-ounce or heavier mesh (non-woven mesh if available).

- Use high-impact mesh on the ground floor and in traffic areas.

- Use silicone sealants for joints.

Drainage EIFS Installation

- Do not break EPS board over sheathing joints. Keep board joints away from window corners.

- Apply base coat in two layers for adequate thickness; ideally, the base coat should be between $1/16$- and $3/32$-in. thick.

- Back-wrap all panel edges with mesh and base coat. Do not leave exposed mesh.

- Apply sealant to base coat, not to finish coat.

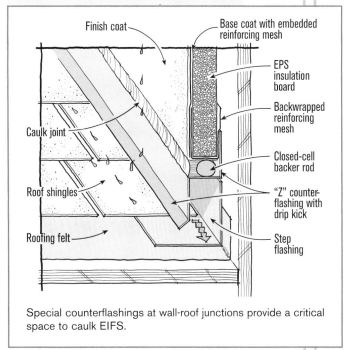

Figure 80. Side-Wall Flashings for EIFS

Finish coat

Base coat with embedded reinforcing mesh

EPS insulation board

Backwrapped reinforcing mesh

Caulk joint

Closed-cell backer rod

Roof shingles

"Z" counter-flashing with drip kick

Roofing felt

Step flashing

Special counterflashings at wall-roof junctions provide a critical space to caulk EIFS.

- Coordinate trades so that flashings and weather barriers are installed in the proper sequence, and be sure that each trade knows its responsibilities.

Repairing Stucco

Hairline Cracks

It's best not to attempt patching hairline cracks with wet stucco; the patch may be more noticeable than the crack. Instead, dust the crack with stucco, as shown in **Figure 82**.

Figure 81. Front-Wall Flashings for EIFS

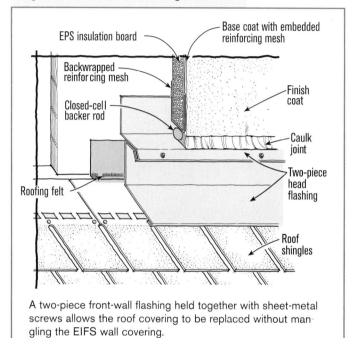

EPS insulation board

Base coat with embedded reinforcing mesh

Backwrapped reinforcing mesh

Finish coat

Closed-cell backer rod

Caulk joint

Two-piece head flashing

Roofing felt

Roof shingles

A two-piece front-wall flashing held together with sheet-metal screws allows the roof covering to be replaced without mangling the EIFS wall covering.

Small Cracks

Slightly larger cracks (up to $1/8$ in.) can be filled with color-matching caulk. To fill the crack, first cover the crack with clear masking tape, and then slit the tape along the crack with a utility knife. Apply the caulk through the slit and remove the tape before the caulk sets.

For cracks $1/8$- to $1/4$-in. wide, use a narrow chisel or large screwdriver to scrape or chip through the color and brown coats to expose the scratch coat. Then, apply an acrylic bonding agent (masking as needed) to strengthen adhesion between the old and new materials. Finally, patch with stucco or special rapid-set patching mortar.

Larger Cracks

When patching wide cracks, wet the surrounding stucco and then apply an acrylic bonding agent. To keep the patch from sagging and shrinking, work the new stucco in layers no more than $1/2$ in. thick. Screed the final layer flush with the existing stucco.

Patching Small Holes

To repair small holes up to 3-in. across, first clean the hole of any loose material and wet the edges. Fill the hole with a rapid-setting mortar mix in one coat. Use a trowel turned on edge to rake off any excess so that the patch is flush with the surrounding wall. After the base hardens, apply the matching texture.

For holes larger than 3 in., use a hammer and cold chisel to carefully chip a tapered edge around the perimeter of the hole. Tapered edges offer more surface area and produce a better bond. A back-cut taper will also lock in the patch. In addition, use wire lath to support the plaster. If possible, nail the metal lath to adjacent studs; otherwise, weave and tie it to the old lath.

Figure 82. Repairing Hairline Cracks

To patch hairline cracks: 1) mask both sides with tape; 2) dab the crack with dry stucco on a small brush; 3) brush off the excess to avoid ridges in the patch; and 4) remove the masking tape and brush again. Overnight condensation will provide enough moisture to cure the dry stucco.

Patching Large Areas

To patch in a large area, the sheathing wrap and lath need to be repaired first. Use a piece of building paper slightly larger than the patch area and lap it to shed water (**Figure 83**).

After the scratch and brown coats have cured, repair the color coat by spraying a light color coating called a "fog coat." Fog consists of cement, color pigment, and lime, but no sand. If possible, use the original stucco

Figure 83. Patching Three-Coat Stucco

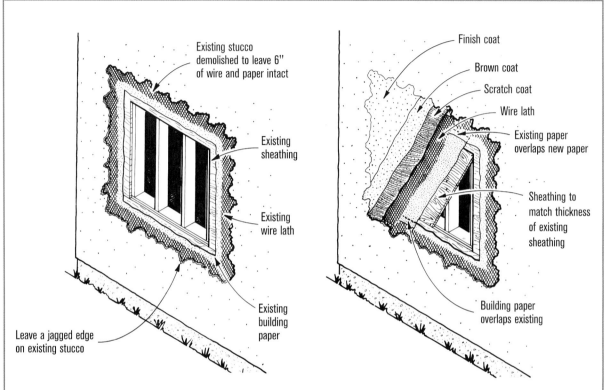

Existing stucco demolished to leave 6" of wire and paper intact

Existing sheathing

Existing wire lath

Existing building paper

Leave a jagged edge on existing stucco

Finish coat

Brown coat

Scratch coat

Wire lath

Existing paper overlaps new paper

Sheathing to match thickness of existing sheathing

Building paper overlaps existing

When patching stucco, chip back at least 6 in. to expose the existing lath and building paper (left). The existing stucco should have a jagged edge to create a less noticeable transition to the new stucco. Match the existing thickness of the sheathing and make sure to lap the building paper so water can drain out (right).

manufacturer's fog coat. Since stucco darkens with age, you may have to add as much as 50% additional pigment if the stucco you're matching is older than six months.

When faced with a large patch like a patio door infill, chances are very high that both the color and texture of the new stucco will not match. Painting the stucco is the only way to assure uniformity of color.

Brick Veneer

Brick Types and Grades

Brick veneer is available in several types and grades, each of which differs in durability, appearance, and dimensional tolerances (**Figures 84** and **85**).

The quality of brick and mortar affects how watertight a wall will be. Softer porous brick absorbs water, while very hard-fired brick absorbs little water but may not bond as well with mortar. Without a good mortar bond, the wall may leak at the joints. Brick with about 6% to 9% water absorption (conforming to ASTM C216) will provide a good bond.

Avoid Used Brick

Under frost/freeze conditions, poor quality bricks will disintegrate rapidly. Old brick may also have contaminants on the surface that will prevent the mortar from bonding.

When laying brick, the mason should pull brick from several cubes at a time, not consume one cube and move onto the next. This will minimize the chance of creating blotchy walls due to normal variations in brick color.

Mortar Types

Mortar bonds masonry units together and seals against air and moisture penetration. It also bonds with joint reinforcement, metal ties, and anchor bolts. For load-bearing applications, mortar performance is as critical as the brick units themselves.

No single mortar type is suited for all applications. For new brick veneer, Type N mortar provides the best combination of strength, workability, and economy.

Figure 84. Brick Grades

	Exposure Grades	Use Conditions
SW	Severe Weathering	All exterior applications
MW	Moderate Weathering	Exterior applications in very mild climates
NW	Negligible Weathering	Interior application only
	Appearance Grades	**Tolerances**
FBX	Face Brick Extra	1/8-in. to 1/4-inch dimension variation
FBS	Face Brick Standard	3/32 to 5/32 dimension variation; minor chips, cracks possible
TBX	Thin Brick Extra	1/8-in. to 1/4-inch dimension variation
TBS	Thin Brick Standard	3/32 to 5/32 dimension variation; minor chips, cracks possible
HBX	Hollow Brick Extra	1/8-in. to 1/4-inch dimension variation
HBS	Hollow Brick Standard	3/32 to 5/32 dimension variation; minor chips, cracks possible

Figure 85. Common Brick Types

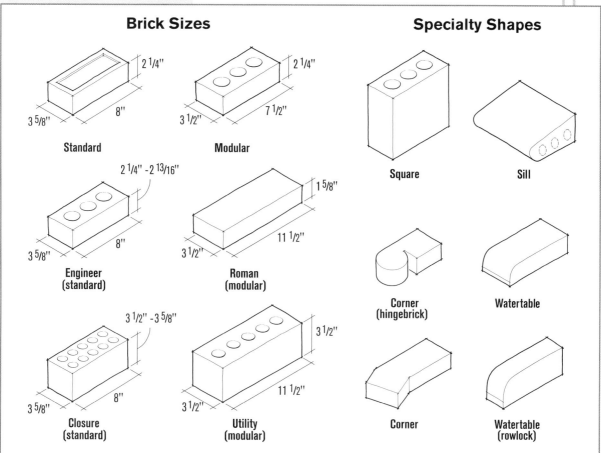

Brick Sizes

Standard

Modular

Engineer (standard)

Roman (modular)

Closure (standard)

Utility (modular)

Specialty Shapes

Square

Sill

Corner (hingebrick)

Watertable

Corner

Watertable (rowlock)

There are literally thousands of brick types to choose from in various shades and textures. Make sure that clients see and approve the brick type before ordering, and that the selected brick works well with the colors and textures of roofing, siding or stucco, window cladding, and trim.

Figure 86. Compressive Strengths of Mortar Types

Mortar Type	Average Compressive Strength at 28 Days (min. psi)
M	2,500
S	1,800
N	750
O	350

When selecting mortar types, a good rule of thumb is to use the mortar with the lowest compressive strength that meets requirements (**Figure 86**).

Mortar Joints

Examples of common mortar joints are shown in **Figure 87**. Each joint provides more than a different architectural appearance; it provides varying degrees of weather resistance, as well. Joints with ledges, such as flush, rake, and struck joints, tend to perform poorly in exterior applications and can allow moisture penetration. Tooled concave or vee joints are recommended for exterior application. The tooling compacts the mortar tightly, minimizing moisture penetration.

Drainage Plane

Because brick is porous, every brick-veneer wall should be designed around a drainage plane. Use well-detailed sheathing wrap over plywood, OSB, foam sheathing, or flexible flashing membrane to waterproof the framing behind it (see "Sheathing Wrap and Flashing," page 8).

Air Space

In commercial work, a 2-in. space is often specified. However, in residential work, a 1-in. gap is acceptable (**Figure 88**). With anything less, there's a good chance that mortar droppings will clog the air space. Be sure to keep the air space open at the top (**Figure 89**).

Weep Holes

Weep holes are an integral part of any drainage plane (**Figure 88**). In brick work, weep holes are usually formed by laying cotton rope or plastic tubing every 16 in., or by leaving an empty head joint (no mortar at the end of the brick) every 24 in. (every third brick). In empty head joints, Cell Vent® (Dur-O-Wal, 630/375-6440, www.dur-o-wal.com) will prevent insects from building nests in the wall, and it looks better than an empty joint.

Structural Support

Brick veneer must be well-supported at the foundation and lintels to prevent settlement. Problems will show up as the building settles at different rates. If differential settlement occurs, step cracks will follow the mortar joints and the crack pattern will grow larger as it goes from the bottom to the top of the wall. To avoid problems:

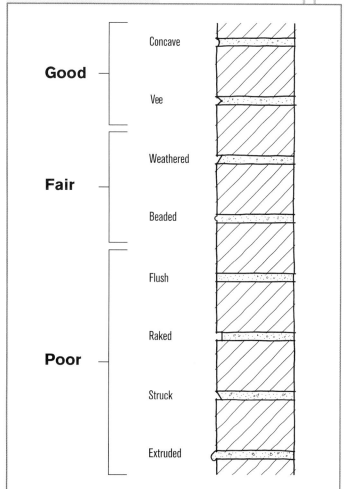

Figure 87. Mortar Joints

The style of the mortar joints in a brick wall influences how well the wall can repel water. Concave and vee joints provide the most weather-resistant joints in exterior walls.

- Support the brick on a stiff, stable ledge or angle bracket (**Figure 90**);

- Tie brick securely to the frame wall.

Figure 88. Drainage Plane for Brick Veneer

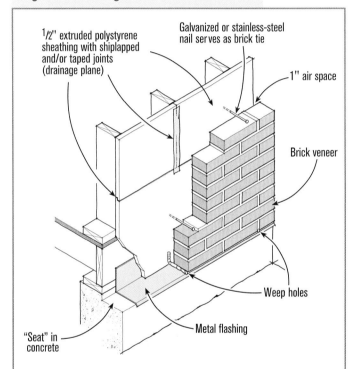

1/2" extruded polystyrene sheathing with shiplapped and/or taped joints (drainage plane)

Galvanized or stainless-steel nail serves as brick tie

1" air space

Brick veneer

Weep holes

Metal flashing

"Seat" in concrete

Brick is very porous and will leak. To prevent water damage to the wall, provide an air space and weep holes to drain water down and out.

Steel Lintels

In residential work, 3x3^1/$_2$x^1/$_4$-in. steel angles will support brick headers for openings less than 6 ft. wide. For larger openings, such as garage doors, use a 5x3^1/$_2$x^1/$_4$-in. angle. The angle should be laid across the opening and then flashed (**Figure 92,** page 96). This metal flashing should tuck under the sheathing wrap 2- to 4-in.

Generally, steel lintels are not attached to the framing. This allows the brick and wood framing, which have different rates of expansion and contraction, to move independently of one another. It is also important to leave space at the end of the lintel for expansion where it is supported on the masonry.

Brick Arches

For standard windows and doors, a segmented or a flat "jack" arch can be used without steel (**Figure 91**). Because the archwork transfers the weight of the wall above the opening to the walls on either side, make sure there is sufficient mass to the left and right of the opening to take the added load. A wide arch placed too near the corner of a house can blow out the corner.

Figure 89. Drainage Plane Details

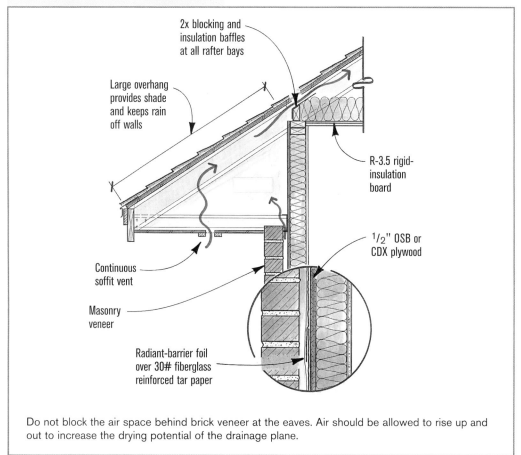

2x blocking and insulation baffles at all rafter bays

Large overhang provides shade and keeps rain off walls

R-3.5 rigid-insulation board

$^1/_2$" OSB or CDX plywood

Continuous soffit vent

Masonry veneer

Radiant-barrier foil over 30# fiberglass reinforced tar paper

Do not block the air space behind brick veneer at the eaves. Air should be allowed to rise up and out to increase the drying potential of the drainage plane.

Flashing Details

In veneer construction, flashing is required at all shelf angles, concrete foundations, and over door and window heads to interrupt the downward flow of water (**Figure 92**).

Flashing Materials

Flashings for brick were traditionally made from copper or lead sheeting. These materials perform well, but their use has steadily decreased because of the cost and the potential for staining and galvanic corrosion.

Aluminum flashings should be used only with extreme caution since the wet and alkaline environment of mortar can corrode the aluminum. Similarly, some galvanized flashings can corrode in fresh mortar, and the galvanized coating may crack during bending and handling.

Flexible flashings work best. They are resilient, durable, and resistant to corrosion (see "Flexible Flashing Materials," page 13). Make sure that flexible flashing membranes are kept covered; UV light will degrade them.

Figure 90. Foundation Support for Brick Veneer

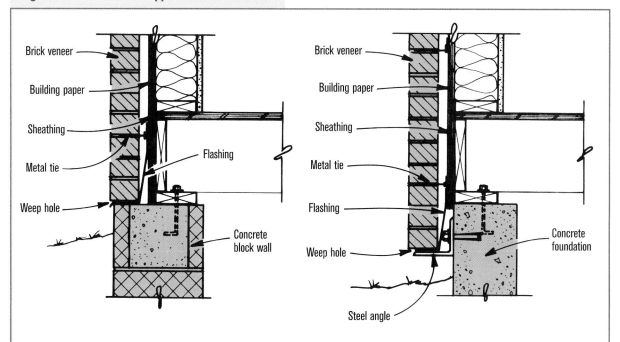

In new construction, build foundation walls wide enough to provide a 4-in. shelf for the brick (left). A stainless-steel angle bolted onto an existing foundation (right) can support a retrofit brick veneer wall up to 14 ft. high. The steel should be installed above-grade, and should be wide enough to support two-thirds the width of the brick.

Figure 91. Brick Arches for Openings

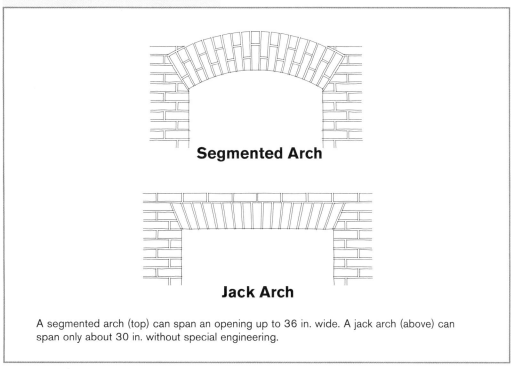

Segmented Arch

Jack Arch

A segmented arch (top) can span an opening up to 36 in. wide. A jack arch (above) can span only about 30 in. without special engineering.

Brick Ties

Brick ties transfer horizontal wind loads on the building to the structural wall framing and the foundation. The ties must be strong enough to resist tensile and compressive forces (**Figure 93**).

For low-rise construction, follow these rules of thumb:

- Use one tie for every $3^1/4$ sq. ft. of wall area, with a maximum spacing of 24 in. on-center. Over a wood-framed wall, this translates to approximately one tie per stud every sixth or seventh course.

- Over a concrete masonry structure or steel-framed wall, use continuous horizontal joint-reinforcement with U-tabs or individual Z-ties.

- For brick veneer over wood fram-ing, use corrosion-resistant corru-gated metal ties, at least 22-gauge, $^7/8$-in. wide, and 6 in. long (**Figure 93**), or 20d galvanized spikes (**Figure 88**, page 92).

Figure 92. Details for Durable Brick Veneer

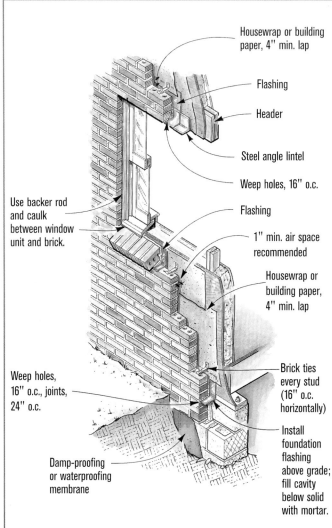

Housewrap or building paper, 4" min. lap

Flashing

Header

Steel angle lintel

Weep holes, 16" o.c.

Flashing

1" min. air space recommended

Housewrap or building paper, 4" min. lap

Use backer rod and caulk between window unit and brick.

Brick ties every stud (16" o.c. horizontally)

Install foundation flashing above grade; fill cavity below solid with mortar.

Weep holes, 16" o.c., joints, 24" o.c.

Damp-proofing or waterproofing membrane

Flashing details are critical for the durability of brick veneer. For best results, use flexible flashings (see also "Flexible Flashing Materials," page 13).

Expansion Joints

Expansion joints in brick masonry will prevent cracking due to thermal movement, moisture-absorption, and load effects. Accumulated movements are usually not large enough in residential construction to warrant expansion joints. However, long walls (over 75 ft.) can have problems.

Repointing Brick

Old brickwork should be repointed to protect it from further damage. Once mortar joints begin to fail, the deterioration can accelerate damage to the brick itself and increase the likelihood of leaks.

Raking Out Mortar

Old mortar should be removed (using a hammer, chisel, and a tuck-point grinder or a pneumatic chisel) to a minimum depth of two-and-a-half times the width of the joint. A depth of about 1 in. deep usually will ensure an adequate bond. Any loose or disintegrated mortar beyond this depth also should be removed. Clean joints carefully; damage to bricks will affect the appearance, and also can lead to accelerated weather damage (**Figure 94**).

Tuck-Pointing

- Dampen the brick and old mortar before filling the joint to control the rate of hardening, but avoid free water or excessive wetting. Too much water will delay the tooling or cause excessive shrinkage; too little water will reduce bond strength.

- Use only prehydrated lime mortar for tuck-pointing. A hard, Portland cement mortar may cause the brick to spall (**Figure 95**). To prehydrate, thoroughly mix dry mortar ingredients. Then add just enough water to produce a very stiff, unworkable mix (it should retain its shape only when pressed into a ball). Let stand for about two hours, and then add enough water to bring it to a good, workable consistency. This will be somewhat stiffer than conventional masonry mortars and will be much easier to work into joints.

- Where existing mortar has been removed to a depth greater than 1 in., compact the new mortar in several 1/4-in.-thick layers to reduce overall shrinkage. Allow each layer time to harden before applying the next layer.

- When the mortar is thumb-print hard, the joint should be tooled to match the existing joint (**Figure 96**). Proper timing of the tooling is important. If tooled when the mortar is too soft, the color will be lighter than expected, and hairline cracks may occur. If tooled too hard, there may be dark streaks called "tool burning," and the mortar will not bond tightly to the brick.

Figure 93. Brick Ties

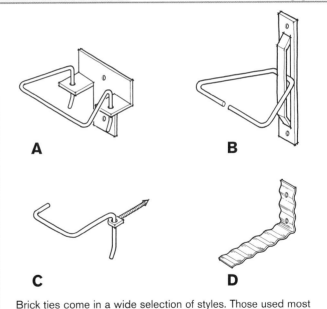

A　　　　　**B**

C　　　　　**D**

Brick ties come in a wide selection of styles. Those used most commonly in residential construction include U-tabs (A and B), Z-ties (C), and corrugated ties (D).

Figure 94. Removing Mortar

Incorrect

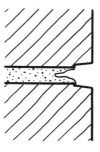

Mortar is not cleaned out to a uniform depth. Edges of brick are damaged by tool or grinder, which creates a wider joint.

Correct

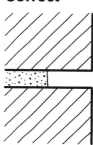

Mortar is cleaned out to a uniform depth — about 1" deep. Edges of brick are undamaged.

When raking joints, remove mortar to a uniform depth (bottom) for maximum bond of the new mortar, and take care not to damage the edges of the brick and create an uneven joint (top).

Cleanup

If repointing work is done carefully, the only cleaning required after tooling will be a small amount of mortar brushed from the edge of the joint with a stiff bristle brush. This is done after the mortar has dried, but before it is fully hardened (one to two hours). Mortar that has hardened can usually be removed with a wooden paddle or, if necessary, a chisel.

Efflorescence, or "bloom," may appear within the first few months after repointing, but it usually disappears through the normal weathering process. If natural processes do not remove the efflorescence, the safest way to remove it is by dry-brushing with stiff natural- or nylon-bristle brushes and water. Usually, muriatic acid is ineffective and it should be avoided. In fact, it can deposit salts, which can lead to additional efflorescence.

Figure 95. Lime vs. Cement Mortar

Lime Mortar

Hot   **Cold**

Portland-Cement Mortar

Hot   **Cold**

With old brick that is soft, it's important to use a soft lime mortar, which will flex with changes of temperature. If a hard, Portland-cement mortar is used, the brick will spall or joints will open up when the brick moves.

Figure 96. Tooling Joints

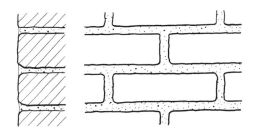

Incorrect
Joints are filled too full. Wide feather edge is susceptible to spalling.

Do not finish mortar joints flush. The thin edges of the mortar where it meets the weathered brick will be weak and may fail.

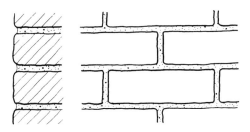

Correct
Joints are slightly recessed, which makes a durable joint.

Caulks and Sealants

Waterproofing details for exterior trim and siding should rely on sheathing wrap and flashing (see page 8) and good design principles (see "Design Principles of Exterior Woodwork," page 26), not on caulk. Caulk is only a first-line defense. Caulk joints accommodate dimensional changes due to climate and settlement, but they should never be the sole means of keeping water out of the wall.

Figure 97. Exterior Caulk Selection Guide

Type	Joint Movement	Life Expectancy	Comments
Silicone	50%	20 yrs.	Very low shrinkage; may be applied over the widest range of temperatures; not paintable; poor adhesion to damp surfaces and to masonry
Polyurethane	25%	20 to 30 yrs.	Best all-purpose caulk; excellent adhesion to most materials; difficult to clean up
Ethylene copolymer	25%	18 to 20 yrs.	Reasonable adhesion to most materials; can be painted
Polysulfide	12 to 25%	20 yrs.	Difficult to handle; may require primer on porous surfaces; wear gloves and maintain ventilation during application
Acrylic latex with silicon	10%	10 to 20 yrs.	Easy to work with; cleans up with water
Acrylic latex	2%	4 to10 yrs	Interior application only; easy to work with; cleans up with water
Butyl rubber	5 to 10%	4 to10 yrs	Poor adhesion on damp surfaces; attracts dirt; difficult to handle
Oil-based	1%	3 to 5 yrs.	Not recommended

Selecting Caulk

There are four types of polymer used to manufacture most high-perform-ance caulks: silicones, polyurethanes, latex acrylics, and the solvent-based "block copolymer" synthetic rubbers. The best type of caulk for the job depends largely on the materials to which the caulk must bond. For the most part, polyurethane caulks provide the best all-around performance for exterior applications, but they are more expensive than most other caulks and can be difficult to clean up (**Figure 97**).

Joint Design

If the joint sealant is too shallow or deep, it will not expand and compress with the movement of the joint. Instead, it may split or rip away from one of the joint surfaces.

Shape

Ideally, caulk joints should be config-ured to span a gap that is half as deep as it is wide (**Figure 98**). The caulk should not bond to the back (three-sided bonding), but only to two sides, so it can flex as it expands and con-tracts.

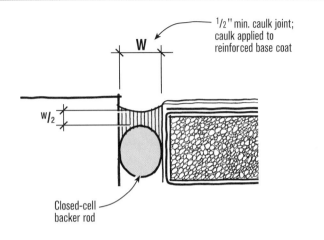

Figure 98. Proper Joint Design

W

$^1/_2$" min. caulk joint; caulk applied to reinforced base coat

$^w/_2$

Closed-cell backer rod

A good caulk joint should bond to only two sides, not to the back. Use backer rod to control the depth, which should be half the width of the joint.

Corner fillets do not move freely and generally peel off the two surfaces. If a joint depends on a caulk sealant, open it up slightly to allow caulk to fill the gap. If a corner is tight, don't caulk it; the caulk will fail faster than any finish applied to it and will only complicate refinishing.

Backer Rod

Backer rod should be used to fill large gaps and control the depth (**Figure 98**). Most backer rod today is made out of foam and comes in diameters from $^1/_4$ in. to 2 in. and up. Choose a backer rod that's just a little larger than the joint so it will stay in place and allow you to control the depth of the sealant.

Foam backer rod comes in open-cell and closed-cell form. Open-cell backer rod compresses more and is easier to work with, but it's like a sponge and can absorb water. In critical areas that may absorb moisture from the substrate, use a closed-cell material.

Bond-breaker tape. The main purpose of backer rod is to keep sealant off the back of the joint, thus preventing three-sided bonding. If the joint is too shallow to fit backer rod, apply bond-breaker tape to the back of the joint.

Applying Caulk

The fine print on the label of most caulk tubes reads: "Apply to clean, dry surfaces. Application temperature: 40°F to 80°F." However, construction sites are never clean, seldom dry, and work doesn't stop when the temperature drops below 40°F. To promote good adhesion, prepare the surface using the following strategies:

- Scrape, chip, brush with a stiff-bristle brush, and dust the inside of the joint, or even blow it out with compressed air.

- Wipe the surface with a strong solvent, such as acetone or methyl ethyl ketone (available in hardware stores and contractor supply houses). These solvents evaporate water and dissolve greasy substances that can retard adhesion.

- Every caulk joint should be tooled. The best tool is a steel spatula (or sculptor's tool) that is slightly smaller than the width of the joint. Try to achieve a smooth, even appearance without squeeze-out on the sides.

- Cut the nozzle of the tube at an angle slightly smaller than the size of the joint.

- In cold weather, keep the caulk warm. If necessary, use an electric heat chest to store tubes. Also, it may be necessary to heat the surface with a hair dryer or a heat gun (just be careful not to strip the paint or start a fire).

Finishes

Success with painted siding and trim starts with an understanding of how the siding will perform under local weather conditions. Next, it's necessary to match the finish to the siding — a given finish performs differently on different types of siding.

Paint Bonding Characteristics of Wood

Avoiding paint problems begins with selecting the best wood available (**Figure 99**). When choosing softwood for exterior siding and trim, begin by looking at the following characteristics:

- **Wood density.** The density of wood is one of the most important factors affecting paint life for a simple reason: "Heavy" woods shrink and swell more than "light" woods (**Figure 99**). Excessive dimensional change constantly stresses paint or a solid-color stain, and may result in early failure. Finishes that don't form a film, such as penetrating stains, are not affected by these dimensional changes.

Figure 99. Paint Holding Ability of Selected Softwoods

	Weight per Cu. Ft. at 8% Moisture Content	Paint-holding Ability (I best, IV worst)
Western red cedar	22.4	I
Redwood	27.4	I
Eastern white pine	24.2	II
Ponderosa pine	27.5	III
Western hemlock	28.7	III
Spruce	26.8	III
Douglas fir	31.0	IV
Red pine	30.8	IV
Southern yellow pine	38.2	IV

Lighter-weight woods shrink and swell less than denser woods, so they tend to hold paint better. Besides being less dense, redwood and cedar have more narrow bands of latewood compared with Southern yellow pine and Douglas fir, which are higher in density and have wide bands of latewood.

- **Flat-grain vs. edge-grain.** Flat-grained lumber shrinks and swells more than edge-grained lumber, so edge-grained (or vertical grain) lumber will usually hold paint better than flat-grained material. Most standard lumber grades contain a high percentage of flat grain.

Figure 100. Suitability and Expected Life of Exterior Wood Finishes

Type of Exterior Wood Surface	Water-Repellent Preservatives and Oil		Semi-Transparent Stain		Paint and Solid-Color Stain		
	Suitability	Expected Life (years)	Suitability	Expected Life (years)	Suitability	Expected Life (years)	
						Paint	Solid-color Stain
SIDING **Cedar & redwood**							
Smooth (vertical grain)	High	1-2	Moderate	2-3	High	4-6	3-5
Roughsawn	High	2-3	High	5-8	Moderate	5-7	4-6
Pine, fir, spruce							
Smooth (flat-grained)	High	1-2	Low	2-3	Moderate	3-5	2-4
Rough (flat-grained)	High	2-3	High	4-7	Moderate	4-6	3-5
Plywood (Douglas fir & Southern Pine)							
Sanded	Very Low	1-2	Low	2-4	Moderate	2-4	2-3
Textured (roughsawn)	Low	2-3	High	4-6	Moderate	4-6	3-5
Medium-density overlay	–	–	–	–	Excellent	6-8	5-7
Hardboard, medium density							
Smooth or Textured	–	–	–	–	High	4-6	3-5
MILLWORK (often pine) **Windows, shutters, doors, exterior trim**	High	–	Moderate	2-3	High	3-6	2-4
DECKING **New (smooth)**	High	1-2	Moderate	2-3	Very Low	2-3	1-2
Weathered (rough)	High	2-3	High	3-4	Very Low	2-3	1-2

Note: These data were compiled from the observations of many researchers. Expected life predictions are for one and two coats of each finish at an average location in the continental United States. Expected life will vary in extreme climates or exposure, such as desert, seashore, and deep woods.

- **Earlywood and latewood.** Earlywood and latewood can be seen as two distinct bands in wood. Latewood is denser, harder, smoother, and darker than earlywood. Although new paint or solid-color stain will adhere well to both earlywood and latewood, old alkyd paints and solid-color stains that have become brittle with age and weathering will peel sooner from the smooth, hard surface of the latewood.

- **Heartwood and sapwood.** Mature trees have a darker central column of wood, called heartwood, surrounded by a lighter cylinder of wood, called sapwood. Heartwood is impregnated with extractives, pitch, and oil, which give the heartwood of some species — such as redwood, cedar, and cypress — a natural resistance to decay and insects. Extractives, however, can sometimes cause discoloration problems as they dissolve in water and are transported to the wood surface.

- **Knots and other irregularities,** such as bark, splits, and pitch pockets also affect paint adhesion. Knots are mainly exposed end grain, which absorbs more finish than flat- and edge-grained lumber. In pine, knots often contain a high percentage of resin, which may cause the paint over the knot to discolor.

Large knots usually check and crack. To reduce the brown stain over knots, apply a primer, such as a pigmented shellac, to block the extractives, and then follow with two top coats.

- **Moisture content** is critical in determining the service life of paint. Allow wood to acclimate to site conditions (see "Conditioning Siding," page 38). Wood above 20% moisture content should never be painted, as the paint will most likely peel.

- **Surface texture.** Paint lasts longer on smooth, edge-grained surfaces than on smooth, flat-grained ones. However, paint will last longest on rough-sawn or rough-sanded wood, whether the wood is edge-grained or flat-grained. Sand smooth siding with 60-grit paper before painting.

Paint vs. Primer

A primer contains a higher ratio of binder to pigment than a topcoat. This forms a protective surface film, seals in extractives, and keeps the wood from unevenly absorbing the topcoat.

The topcoat, on the other hand, contains more pigment but less binder. This is necessary to shield the wood from the sun's ultraviolet rays.

Water and ultraviolet light are the biggest enemies of exterior wood, but a good paint job will protect against both. Binder seals out water, while the pigments form a shield against ultraviolet light. No single coating has enough binder and pigment to do both. However, the combination of primer and topcoat forms the most durable finish.

- **Repainting.** Where the existing paint is chalky, oily, or poorly adhered, use an oil-based or alkyd primer. Ideally, such areas should be sanded to bare wood before priming; but when this is not practical, an oil-based primer will provide the most secure base for the finish coat.

- **Priming tannin-heavy woods.** Oil-based primers also perform better in blocking the tannin stains characteristic of cedar and redwood.

- **Back-priming.** Paints do not penetrate the wood deeply, but form a film on the surface. This film can blister or peel if the wood becomes wet. Without back-priming, the back of the siding absorbs more moisture than the front, leading to cupping, warping, or even paint failure as the moisture looks for a way to escape.

Oil-Based vs. Latex Paints

The most durable house paints are the all-acrylic latex paints. Although oil-based paints usually provide the best protection from liquid water and water vapor, they are not necessarily the most durable because they become brittle over time. Latex paints, particularly the acrylic paints, remain flexible with age. Even though latex paints allow more water vapor to pass through, they hold up better by swelling and shrinking with the wood.

Glossy vs. Flat Paint

Paints are available in different degrees of gloss, including flat, matte, semi-gloss, and gloss. Generally, high-gloss paints contain more paint resin and less pigment, and perform better and last longer than the low-gloss or flat paints. Flat paints tend to pick up dirt and absorb water more readily than the high-gloss paints. Because of this, mildew growth is often greater on the flat paints.

Solid-Color Stains

Solid-color stains are essentially thin paints, not true stains. Solid-color stains have a higher concentration of pigment than semitransparent penetrating stains but a somewhat lower concentration of pigment than standard paints. So solid-color stains cover the wood's natural color while retaining the wood's surface texture.

Solid-color stains will not last as long as paints (**Figure 100**, page 104), but often they are the finish of choice on textured or rough-sawn siding products. They also can be applied over existing paints and solid-color stains, and normally leave a flat finish appearance. Like paints, solid-color stains protect wood against UV degradation.

Clear Exterior Finishes

A penetrating water-repellent preservative contains a preservative (a fungicide), a small amount of wax (or similar water repellent), a resin or drying oil, and a solvent (such as turpentine, mineral spirits, or paraffinic oil). Some may be lightly pigmented, and waterborne formulations are also available.

Unpigmented, or clear, exterior finishes provide minimal protection for wood. They can reduce warping and checking, prevent water staining at the edges and ends of wood siding, and help control mildew growth. Wood treated with preservative is easily refinished and usually requires minimal surface prep.

Paintable water-repellent preservative (such as DAP Woodlife II®,) is a good treatment for bare wood before priming and painting. This pretreatment keeps rain or dew from penetrating the wood, especially at joints and on end-grain, thus decreasing the shrinking and swelling of the wood. As a result, less stress is placed on the paint film and its service life is extended.

Penetrating Oils

Most penetrating oil-based and alkyd-based finishes available contain linseed or tung oil. These oils must have a mildewcide; otherwise, they serve as a food source for mildew. Oils also perform better if a water repellent, such as wax, is included in the formulation. All these oil systems will protect wood, but their average lifetime may be only one to three years.

Semi-Transparent Stains

Semi-transparent penetrating stains are pigmented water-repellent preservatives with a high resin content. Their life expectancy may vary from three to six years, depending on the texture of the wood surface and the quantity of stain applied.

Solvent-borne stains (oil- or alkyd-based) penetrate the wood surface to a degree, are porous, and do not form a surface film like paint. They will not trap moisture that may encourage decay, and they will not blister or peel even if moisture penetrates the wood. Better-quality solvent-borne penetrating stains contain a fungicide (preservative or mildewcide), a stabilizer to protect against ultraviolet radiation (an absorber), and a water repellent.

Waterborne stains (latex-based) do not penetrate the wood surface like their oil-based counterparts. Newer latex formulations are being developed that may provide some penetrating characteristics.

Figure 101. Application of Exterior Wood Finishes

Finish	Initial Application		Maintenance Application	
	Prep	Amount	Prep	Timing
Water-Repellent Preservative	Apply to bare wood only	1 coat prior to painting; avoid wax build-up on surface	Brush to remove surface dirt	1-3 yrs.
Oils (with or without preservative)	Apply to bare wood only	2 coats	Pressure wash	1-3 yrs. or when preferred
Semi-Transparent Stain	Apply to bare wood only	2 coats; use caution to avoid lap marks	Pressure wash	3-6 yrs. or when preferred
Clear Varnish	Apply over 1 coat semitransparent stain to extend service life	3 coats	Clean, sand and stain bleached areas; apply 2 more coats	2 yrs. or when finish breaks down
Paint and Solid-Color Stain	Apply over 1 coat water-repellent preservative and 1 coat primer	2 top coats	Clean and apply top coat, or scrape to remove and repeat initial application	7-10 yrs. for paint; 3-7 yrs. for solid-color stain

Landscape Protection

To protect any plants during a job, saturate the ground and soak all the leaves with water. Then cover the plants with woven poly tarps to shed the bleach solution. Do not use plastic sheeting; the plants must breathe.

After spraying, rinse everything (including the windows and woodwork) thoroughly with water. The siding should dry for two or more days before applying the clear finish.

When using a cleaning solution containing bleach, cover any brass, copper, or aluminum fixtures to avoid corrosion. Also cover any stained or painted trim.

Surface Prep

Water-based finishes require more thorough surface preparation, cleaning, and careful application than oil-based finishes. Remove any loose paint, and clean any dirty or oily surfaces.

Cleaning Siding Surfaces

Dirty siding will require a good cleaning (a detergent wash followed by power washing and thorough drying) to remove chalk and dirt. For most surfaces, use Spic-and-Span® powdered cleaner. On a very oily surface, use painter's naptha.

Filling Nail Holes

Use hot-dipped galvanized finish nails for all trim work that will be filled. The material used to fill nail holes depends on the time available and the type of exterior finish:

Linseed oil-based filler, such as DAP Painter's Putty® (Dap Inc.; 800/543-3840, www.dap.com), works well under an oil-based primer. Add "whiting" (a thickening powder available through paint suppliers) to this somewhat gooey putty to make it more workable. However, it's important that the putty be allowed to dry for a few days before primer is applied.

Exterior spackle. If an oil or latex primer will be applied the same day, use an exterior spackle, such as UGL 222 Spackling Paste (United Gilsonite Laboratories; 800/272-3235, www.ugl.com). Exterior spackle shrinks as it dries, but the hole can be "overloaded" to account for this shrinkage. Sand any proud material flush after it dries.

Epoxy. Where a latex primer will be applied immediately after the holes are filled, use a quick-hardening, two-part filler, such as Bondo®.

Applying Exterior Finishes

Different finishes require different amounts of finish (**Figure 101**, page 108).

Spraying vs. Brushing

While spray guns deliver paint quickly, it is nearly impossible to spray the paint uniformly on uneven surfaces. The best solution for almost any siding is to use a sprayer to get the paint on the wall, and then brush it out evenly and on all surfaces and work it into joints.

Whether brushing, rolling, or spraying, keep a wet edge to prevent lap marks. This may mean painting smaller areas at a time.

Applying Stain and Clear Finishes

For the longest-lasting results, install the siding with the rough side out. Then apply two coats of a lightly-pigmented, semitransparent, oil-based stain that contains a water repellent and a preservative or mildewcide. Apply the first coat and let it soak into the wood 20 to 60 minutes and then apply the second coat. If you allow the first coat to dry, the second coat can-

not penetrate into the wood. About an hour after applying the second coat, use a cloth, sponge, or dry brush to remove any excess stain. Otherwise, the stain that does not penetrate into the wood will form an unsightly film and glossy spots.

Preserving a Natural Wood Finish

Wood siding turns gray because of two factors: the degradation by sun and water of the outermost layer of wood cells, which turn gray as their natural oils dry out, and tiny mildew spores that grow on the wood's surface.

Clear finishes with UV inhibitors will slow the weathering process, but will need to be reapplied every two years or so. Eventually, the color will change. After that, the only option is to approximate the color of new wood by putting on a cedar-tone stain.

Restoring Natural Color

If wood siding is weathered and discolored, the new look can be restored temporarily by cleaning off the dirt and mildew with a solution of one-third cup liquid household detergent (be sure it is ammonia-free), one quart liquid household bleach (containing 4% to 5% sodium hypochlorite), and three quarts warm water. Follow this up with a water rinse, and then use an oxalic acid bleach solution made with about a half pound of oxalic acid per gallon of water. Be sure to rinse with water again. This oxalic acid bleach solution will draw out the tannins in the wood and revive the orange tone of the cedar. Again, be sure to cover plants to protect them from the bleach (see "Landscape Protection," page 109).

Finishes for Shingles and Shakes

Cedar shingles are naturally resistant to insect damage and decay, so they can be left unfinished to weather naturally. However the "natural" look may be less uniform and darker than desired, depending on the wood and its exposure to sun and moisture. Other finishing options include paints, stains, bleaching oils, and various clear preservatives.

Left unfinished, cedar shingles will weather to colors ranging from silver gray to dark brown and even black where there is excessive moisture and limited sunshine. Redwood left unfinished tends to turn black. To ensure a uniform weathered appearance, apply a bleaching oil. A lightly pigmented stain will produce a similar result, offering protection while allowing the natural characteristics of the wood to show through.

Other options include heavy-bodied stains or traditional paints, which should be applied only to thoroughly dry material. The texture of a shingle provides good adhesion for paints and stains.

Painting Stucco

When painting stucco:

- Newly applied stucco should be allowed about 30 days to cure before painting, depending on the weather conditions.

- Existing stucco surfaces should be power-washed and allowed to thoroughly dry before painting. Do not use a water blaster, as the pressure can do severe damage to the stucco.

- Stucco should be painted only with acrylic-based paints with adequate vapor transmission characteristics, as these prevent new moisture-related problems within the house.

Painting Fiber-Cement

Fiber-cement siding does not expand and contract with humidity changes like wood siding does, so it holds paint very well. If the siding is already painted and the paint is in good condition, clean the surface, and then apply at least two coats of high-quality acrylic latex paint.

Priming may not be necessary if the old paint is in good condition (free from peeling, cracking, flaking, etc.). However, if the old paint is glossy, or there are bare spots, it may be best to prime first. Match the primer to the paint of the same brand.

Painting Asbestos Siding

Old asbestos-cement shingles behave like fiber-cement. In general, they take and hold paint well. If the shingles are in good shape, follow the guidelines for fiber-cement.

If some of the siding is deteriorated, showing loose fibers or broken edges, special precautions may be required. Aggressive scraping or sanding of loose paint is not advised since this could release asbestos fibers.